LOVE'S ASPECTS

The World's
Great Love Poems

LOVE'S ASPECTS

DOUBLEDAY & COMPANY, Inc.

The World's Great Love Poems

Selected by JEAN GARRIGUE

Arranged and
with an Introduction
by NANCY SULLIVAN

Drawings by NELL BLAINE

Garden City, New York

Léonie Adams. "Caryatid," from *Poems: A Selection*. Copyright 1954 by Léonie Adams. By permission of Funk & Wagnalls, Inc.

Conrad Aiken. "Imprimis," "My love, I have betrayed you seventy times," "The Quarrel," "The Lovers," "The Accomplices," from *Collected Poems* by Conrad Aiken. Copyright 1953 by Conrad Aiken. Reprinted by permission of Oxford University Press, Inc.

Anna Akhmatova. "The Guest," from *Selected Poems* by Anna Akhmatova, translated by Richard McKane. Translation copyright © 1969 by Richard McKane. By permission of Penguin Books Ltd.

Yehuda Amichai. "A Pity, We Were Such a Good Invention," from *Poems*. Copyright 1968 by Yehuda Amichai, English translation copyright 1968, 1969 by Assia Gutmann. By permission of Harper & Row, Publishers.

Hans Christian Andersen. "The Pearl," from *A Second Book of Danish Verse*, translated by Charles Wharton Stork. Published by The American-Scandinavian Foundation and Princeton University Press, 1947. By permission of the copyright holders.

George Barker. "Sonnet to My Mother," from *Collected Poems*. Copyright © 1957, 1962, 1965 by George Granville Barker. Reprinted by permission of October House, Inc., and Faber & Faber, Ltd.

Charles Baudelaire. "The Little Old Women," translated by Barbara Gibbs, from Angel Flores, editor: *An Anthology of French Poetry from Nerval to Valéry in English Translation*. By permission of Angel Flores.

iv

v

xii

CONTENTS

xv

SECTION 3

SECTION 5

xxiv

SECTION 8

XXV

xxvii

xxix

INTRODUCTION

THE COUNTRY of love is located in the imagination. Its landscape is international, its concerns timeless. The calendars of this country calculate the rising and falling of love's ardor, not months, years or centuries. Its clocks tabulate midnights or dawns. Its poetry fuses bliss and anguish, the twin elements of Love.

The politics of daily living does not interest the maker of love poems. Quite the contrary, so that a love poem by Sappho or Catullus or Shakespeare might today be fresher and more faithful to the basic subject than one being written at this very hour. The *when* is incidental, the *why* elastic and multifaceted.

Is there a difference between a love poem and a poem about love? In a love poem, love is not merely the subject of the poem but its essence. In a very real sense, the act of making such a poem is an act of love: the subject is love, the theme is love, the poet is in love in his poem if not with it. The poem we read is as intimate as a kiss.

Writing and reading about love, one is aware of several paradoxes. The description of love is necessarily a poor substitute for the experience. It may be that the greatest loves have never been celebrated in any poem and that the best poems have been written after the love they sing has cooled. Great art and intense passion may not exist simultaneously. One may be a substitute for the other. But across the several centuries, love poetry continues to be written. Perhaps at heart it is the supreme artistic attempt to span the ideal and the real. The poet who is subject to his age selects a language, convention, and form which seem appropriate, ranging from the control of a sonnet or villanelle to entirely free verse. What unites love poets burns fiercely beneath their apparent differences: the wish to describe in song being transported by passion. This they hope to share with us.

In some respects the general theme of love in poetry follows the pattern of such other great themes as faith, innocence, death, or their opposites. The inspiration and basic impetus are the same in every generation, but the fashion of the resulting work reflects the climate of the times. Poetic celebration of patriotism or faith is somewhat more private today than it was for Spenser, Milton, or Tennyson. One might also say that it is certainly unnecessary to rewrite *The Faerie Queene, Paradise Lost,* or *In Memoriam.* The tradition of courtly love and the grand sonnet sequence are as established in literary tradition as the epic and the spiritual meditation. The manner of our own times has not diminished the intensity of love, but the emphasis has shifted from faith to irony.

The selection of poems for an anthology of love poems is both a delightful and devastating task. There are more good love poems in this world than any one book can house. Then too, the intensity of an anthology composed solely of love poems as I have attempted to define one could prove overwhelming. Paging through this anthology, it will become apparent that Jean Garrigue's intention in selecting poems for it was to include love poems dealing with the bond between human beings involved in the most intense of relationships along with an occasional poem or letter—bawdy, witty, platonic, metaphysical, physical—*about* love. Her final choices reflect her own unique personality and impeccable taste.

She weighed, for example, the omission of many extraordinary longer love poems in order to include a great variety of shorter ones. The selections in this anthology represent the rare tilt of Jean Garrigue's intuitive good and special taste and her wide knowledge of a broad spectrum of poetry from both the English-American tradition as well as the Classical and European. One will find here familiar poems next to less well known but equally exciting ones.

The inclusion of translations demonstrates her theory that Baudelaire, say, or a Provencal poet touched on a theme of love as no one else did. In every case, however, the translation stands in its own right as a successful poem in English.

The arrangement of such a wealth of poems presents its own peculiar problems. Jean Garrigue considered several possibilities: arrangement by subject matter under such headings as "Lineaments of Gratified Desire," "The Open Ulcer of my Heart," "The Expense of Spirit in a Waste of Shame," or something similar. Or another possibility, the tracing of the stages of a love affair as Stendahl speaks of it in his *Essay on Love,* or a division of the anthology into four sections to represent the seasons of love with lines taken from Shakespeare's sonnets as subtitles. The stage of editing she had reached at the time of her death left a manuscript tentatively arranged in four sections reflecting the characteristics of the seasons of the year. All of the poems in the present volume were chosen by her.

My arrangement of the poems is a compromise which takes these earlier ideas into account. The present anthology is divided into twelve sections representing the rising and falling action of the seasons of the year, the twelve hours from the high noon of love to its darkest midnight, or the twelve months of the year which symbolize in a similar pattern the rising and falling of love's cycle. This is not to imply, however, that one cannot experience a rapture in winter!

The subtitles are from poems by Jean Garrigue. In addition I have included seven of her own poems instead of the single one she had planned to include ("Incantatory Poem") on the grounds that she was herself one of the best love poets in her own time. Naturally, any such arrangement is somewhat arbitrary since poems are not written to fit into a category but to break out of one. And finally, the poems themselves, not the pattern they create or fail to create, are what really matter. Nell Blaine's striking and lucid drawings evoke, it seems to me, the mood of clarity and mystery which characterizes the best love poems of any period.

It is a pleasure to acknowledge the help of several friends whose kind advice and interest have greatly aided me in the completion of this anthology: Aileen Ward, Nancy A. J. Potter, Marjorie Garrigue Smith, Jane Mayhall, Leslie Katz, and my sensitive and patient editor, Marjorie Goldstein.

NANCY SULLIVAN

JEAN GARRIGUE

(1912–1972)

JEAN GARRIGUE's enthusiasms were intense. She loved poetry, music, cats, birds, ferris wheels, the circus, flowers and weeds, the ballet, trees both in bloom and bare, kites, the sea, the Staten Island ferry. She enjoyed travel as experience and memory; her verse meditations upon places real and imagined are uniquely landscaped. One of her most forceful poems, "The Grand Canyon," was written in the last year of her life after a first trip to the canyon.

Jean Garrigue was born in Indiana, graduated from the University of Chicago, and later earned an M.F.A. from the University of Iowa. After that, New York City became her home and her haven punctuated by intermittent trips to Europe. She was a vital part of the rich renaissance in painting and poetry in New York during the forties and fifties. A fierce defender of her city, she was later exasperated by its inability to cope with the smog and soot, those enemies of an ecological progress she wholly supported.

Jean Garrigue was the author of seven books of poetry, one of these, *Country Without Maps*, was nominated for a National Book Award. *Studies for an Actress*, her last book of poems, was published posthumously. Her prose work included a novella, *The Animal Hotel*; *Chartres and Prose Poems*; short stories; reviews and critical studies. In addition, she taught and read at a number of leading colleges and universities throughout the country.

Jean Garrigue's great physical beauty was matched by her ability to translate into words the pleasurable essence of bliss. Her own love poems are brilliant exercises in tension, studies in the inevitability of passion, "Love stamps its foot but cannot slip the knot." They sing the brilliant mystery of first discovery, "When everything had excellence at once," and the waning afterlight, "The nothing else can equal after it." It was predictable that critics in her lifetime would praise her verbal elegance and inventive rhetoric above the tough truths she knew so well about the joy and disappointment of love, "And though the smoke is gone there is some fire / In saying so."

She was at work in choosing poems for this anthology until the month of her death in December 1972. The pleasure she took in this work is evident in the rich, authentic, fresh tone of this collection which becomes a fitting tribute to her candor and talents.

LOVE'S ASPECTS

The World's
Great Love Poems

April is in my mistress' face,
And July in her eyes hath place.
Within her bosom, a warm September;
But in her heart, a cold December.

                              Anonymous

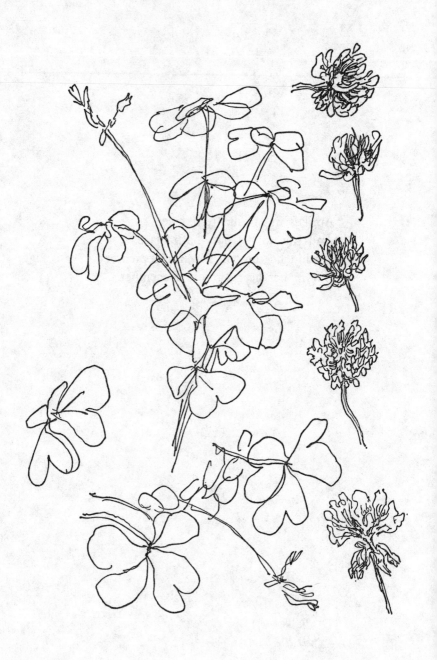

1

"Love loves what love is
Nor can it change that . . ."

For Anybody's Martyr's Song

What's love that's always strong?
Beasts from the Antipodes, spring down!
And hoydens leap like lions over beaches!
Love is the friend whose faithfulness is wit,
Is best your mimic when you tongue-tied vow,
Aloof when you win and surly when you stammer,
Cries I do not understand you, and
Corrects your right answer.

Indulges with contempt your sweet tooth at the fair,
Gives you fearful rides on the roller coaster,
Greets you like a sovereign when you've come
An hour, but puts the green toad in your bed
Just as soon thereafter.
Your sober love turns tomcat in the bar.

Children hate school, soldiers discipline,
Love hates love but what's the good of that?
O the sweet cry, the dark eye!
Love stamps its foot but cannot slip the knot.

Nor can remove the leopard's spot
Nor ever dye the wolf white,
Love loves what love is
Nor can it change that.

Jean Garrigue

5

The Definition of Love

My love is of a birth as rare
As 'tis for object strange and high:
It was begotten by Despair,
Upon Impossibility.

II

Magnanimous Despair alone
Could show me so divine a thing,
Where feeble Hope could ne'er have flown,
But vainly flapped its tinsel wing.

III

And yet I quickly might arrive
Where my extended soul is fixed;
But Fate does iron wedges drive,
And always crowds itself betwixt.

IV

For Fate with jealous eye does see
Two perfect loves, nor lets them close;
Their union would her ruin be,
And her tyrannic power depose.

V

And therefore her decrees of steel
Us as the distant poles have placed,
Though love's whole world on us doth wheel,
Not by themselves to be embraced,

VI

Unless the giddy heaven fall,
And earth some new convulsion tear;
And, us to join, the world should all
Be cramped into a planisphere.

VII

As lines, so loves, oblique, may well
Themselves in every angle greet;
But ours so truly parallel,
Though infinite, can never meet.

VIII

Therefore the love which us doth bind,
But Fate so enviously debars,
Is the conjunction of the mind
And opposition of the stars.

Andrew Marvell

The Lover to His Lady

My girl, thou gazest much
    Upon the golden skies.
Would I were Heaven! I would behold
    Thee then with all mine eyes.

George Turberville

Seven Seals

Since this is the last night I keep you home.
Come, I will consecrate you for the journey.

Rather I had you would not go. Nay come,
I will not again reproach you. Lie back
And let me love you a long time ere you go.
For you are sullen-hearted still, and lack
The will to love me. But even so
I will set a seal upon you from my lip,
Will set a guard of honour at each door,
Seal up each channel out of which might slip
Your love for me.

          I kiss your mouth. Ah, love,
Could I but seal its ruddy, shining spring
Of passion, parch it up, destroy, remove
Its softly-stirring crimson welling-up
Of kisses! Oh, help me, God! Here at the source
I'd lie for ever drinking and drawing in
Your fountains, as heaven drinks from out their course
The floods.

        I close your ears with kisses
And seal your nostrils, and round your neck you'll wear—
Nay, let me work—a delicate chain of kisses.
Like beads they go around, and not one misses
To touch its fellow on either side.

         And there
Full mid-between the champaign of your breast
I place a great and burning seal of love
Like a dark rose, a mystery of rest
On the slow bubbling of your rhythmic heart.

8

Nay, I persist, and very faith shall keep
You integral to me. Each door, each mystic port
Of egress from you I will seal and steep
In perfect chrism.

                    Now it is done. The mort
Will sound in heaven before it is undone.
But let me finish what I have begun
And shirt you now invulnerable in the mail
Of iron kisses, kisses linked like steel.
Put greaves upon your thighs and knees, and frail
Webbing of steel on your feet. So you shall feel
Ensheathed invulnerable with me, with seven
Great seals upon your outgoings, and woven
Chain of my mystic will wrapped perfectly
Upon you, wrapped in indomitable me.

                         D. H. Lawrence

The Happiness of a Flea

How happier is that flea
Which in thy breast doth play,
Than that pied butterfly
Which courts the flame, and in the same doth lie.
That hath a light delight,
Poor fool, contented only with a sight;
When this doth sport, and swell with dearest food,
And if he die, he, knight-like, dies in blood.

                    Torquato Tasso
                    Translated from the Italian
                    by W. Drummond

The Passionate Shepherd
to His Love

Come live with me, and be my love,
And we will all the pleasures prove
That valleys, groves, hills and fields,
Woods, or steepy mountain yields.

And we will sit upon the rocks,
Seeing the shepherds feed their flocks
By shallow rivers, to whose falls
Melodious birds sing madrigals.

And I will make thee beds of roses,
And a thousand fragrant posies;
A cap of flowers, and a kirtle,
Embroider'd all with leaves of myrtle.

A gown made of the finest wool,
Which from our pretty lambs we pull;
Fair lined slippers for the cold,
With buckles of the purest gold.

A belt of straw and ivy buds,
With coral clasps and amber studs,
An if these pleasures may thee move,
Come live with me, and be my love.

The shepherd swains shall dance and sing
For thy delight each May-morning:
If these delights thy mind may move,
Then live with me, and be my love.

Christopher Marlowe

"My lovers suffocate me"

My lovers suffocate me,
Crowding my lips, thick in the pores of my skin,
Jostling me through streets and public halls, coming naked to me
    at night,
Crying by day *Ahoy!* from the rocks of the river, swinging and
    chirping over my head,
Calling my name from flower-beds, vines, tangled underbrush,
Lighting on every moment of my life,
Bussing my body with soft balsamic busses,
Noiselessly passing handfuls out of their hearts and giving them
    to be mine.

                                  Walt Whitman

Up Tailes All

        Begin with a kisse,
        Go on too with this:
And thus, thus, thus let us smother
        Our lips for a while,
        But let's not beguile
Our hope of one for the other.

        This play, be assur'd,
        Long enough has endur'd,
Since more and more is exacted;
        For love he doth call
        For his Uptailes all;
And that's the part to be acted.

                            Robert Herrick

"Who shall have my faire lady?"

Who shall have my faire lady?
Who shall have my faire lady?
Who but I, who but I, who but I?
Under the levis grene!

The fairest man
That best love can,
Dandirly, dandirly,
Dandirly, dan,
Under the levis grene.

Anonymous

Song

Oh, with the hunger of the sea, forever born anew,
    With great waves straining, striving, pouring toward the
        strand,
The sea of my heart's life in exultation moves toward you,
        toward you,
Unreachable far land!

You are that land; you are the sea of which I am a part
    In love and dream. Like waves beating upon
Trembling shores, the shock and smiting of your loveliness
        upon my heart,
O dear and lovely one.

John Hall Wheelock

12

"The animal moment, when he sorted out her tail"

The animal moment, when he sorted out her tail
in a rump session with the vivid hostess
whose guests had finally gone,
was stronger, though so limited, though failed
all normal impulse before her interdiction, yes,
and Henry gave in.

I'd like to have your baby, but, she moaned,
I'm married. Henry muttered to himself
So am I and was glad
to keep chaste. If this lady he had had
scarcely could he have have ever forgiven himself
and how would he have atoned?

—Mr Bones, you strong on moral these days, hey?
It's good to be faithful but it ain't natural,
as you knows.
—I knew what I knew when I knew when I was astray,
all those bright painful years, forgiving all
but when Henry & his wives came to blows.

John Berryman

The Canonization

For Godsake hold your tongue, and let me love,
   Or chide my palsie, or my gout,
My five gray haires, or ruin'd fortune flout,
    With wealth your state, your minde with Arts improve,
     Take you a course, get you a place,

Observe his honour, or his grace,
Or the Kings reall, or his stamped face
   Contemplate, what you will, approve,
   So you will let me love.

Alas, alas, who's injur'd by my love?
   What merchants ships have my sighs drown'd?
Who saies my teares have overflow'd his ground?
   When did my colds a forward spring remove?
     When did the heats which my veines fill
     Adde one more to the plaguie Bill?
Soldiers finde warres, and Lawyers finde out still
   Litigious men, which quarrels move,
   Though she and I do love.

Call us what you will, wee are made such by love;
   Call her one, mee another flye,
We'are Tapers too, and at our owne cost die,
   And wee in us finde the' Eagle and the Dove.
     The Phoenix ridle hath more wit
     By us, we two being one, are it.
So to one neutrall thing both sexes fit,
   Wee dye and rise the same, and prove
   Mysterious by this love.

Wee can dye by it, if not live by love,
   And if unfit for tombes and hearse
Our legend bee, it will be fit for verse;
   And if no peece of Chronicle wee prove,
     We'll build in sonnets pretty roomes;
     As well a well wrought urne becomes
The greatest ashes, as halfe-acre tombes,
   And by these hymnes, all shall approve
   Us *Canoniz'd* for Love:

And thus invoke us; You whom reverend love
　　Made one anothers hermitage;
You, to whom love was peace, that now is rage;
　　Who did the whole worlds soule contract, and drove
　　　Into the glasses of your eyes
　　(So made such mirrors, and such spies,
That they did all to you epitomize),
　　Countries, Townes, Courts: Beg from above
　　A patterne of your love!

John Donne

The Young Girl

What can the spirit believe?—
It takes in the whole body;
I, on coming to love,
Make that my study.

We are one, and yet we are more,
I am told by those who know,—
At times content to be two.
Today I skipped on the shore,
My eyes neither here nor there,
My thin arms to and fro,
A bird my body,
My bird-blood ready.

Theodore Roethke

Queen-Anne's-Lace

Her body is not so white as
anemone petals nor so smooth—nor
so remote a thing. It is a field
of the wild carrot taking
the field by force; the grass
does not raise above it.
Here is no question of whiteness,
white as can be, with a purple mole
at the center of each flower.
Each flower is a hand's span
of her whiteness. Wherever
his hand has lain there is
a tiny purple blemish. Each part
is a blossom under his touch
to which the fibres of her being
stem one by one, each to its end,
until the whole field is a
white desire, empty, a single stem,
a cluster, flower by flower,
a pious wish to whiteness gone over—
or nothing.

William Carlos Williams

Elements of Night

Shelter was possible. Instead
we chose a sea ledge as our bed.
No conflict could be great enough
wanting to do all we could for love.
We said to the elements of night:
"The agitation at your core,
ingots of heaven thrust into
combustions to dissolve,
what causes particles to split,
the conflict causing you to seethe,
we seek in each other's arms
to burn with and appease."
Silver water foamed at our feet.
Starlight wrapped itself
around us like a haze:
the same white breath
steaming from our nakedness.

Arthur Gregor

"I knew a woman"

I knew a woman, lovely in her bones,
When small birds sighed, she would sigh back at them;
Ah, when she moved, she moved more ways than one:
The shapes a bright container can contain!
Of her choice virtues only gods should speak,
Or English poets who grew up on Greek
(I'd have them sing in chorus, cheek to cheek).

How well her wishes went! She stroked my chin,
She taught me Turn, and Counter-turn, and Stand;
She taught me Touch, that undulant white skin;
I nibbled meekly from her proffered hand;
She was the sickle; I, poor I, the rake,
Coming behind her for her pretty sake
(But what prodigious mowing we did make).

Love likes a gander, and adores a goose:
Her full lips pursed, the errant note to seize;
She played it quick, she played it light and loose;
My eyes, they dazzled at her flowing knees;
Her several parts could keep a pure repose,
Or one hip quiver with a mobile nose
(She moved in circles, and those circles moved).

Let seed be grass, and grass turn into hay:
I'm martyr to a motion not my own;
What's freedom for? To know eternity.
I swear she cast a shadow white as stone.
But who would count eternity in days?
These old bones live to learn her wanton ways:
(I measure time by how a body sways).

Theodore Roethke

. . . My head is puzzled this morning, and I scarce know what I shall say though I am full of a hundred things. 'T is certain I would rather be writing to you this morning, notwithstanding the alloy of grief in such an occupation, than enjoy any other pleasure, with health to boot, unconnected with you. Upon my soul I have loved you to the extreme. I wish you could know the Tenderness with which I continually brood over your different aspects of countenance, action and dress. I see you come down in the morning: I see you meet me at the Window—I see every thing over again eternally that I ever have seen. If I get on the pleasant clue I live in a sort of happy misery, if on the unpleasant 'tis miserable misery. You complain of my illtreating you in word thought and deed—I am sorry,—at times I feel bitterly sorry that I ever made you unhappy—my excuse is that those words have been wrung from me by the sha[r]pness of my feelings. At all events and in any case I have been wrong; could I believe that I did it without any cause, I should be the most sincere of Penitents. I could give way to my repentant feelings now, I could recant all my suspicions, I could mingle with you heart and Soul though absent, were it not for some parts of your Letters. Do you suppose it possible I could ever leave you? You know what I think of myself and what of you. You know that I should feel how much it was my loss and how little yours . . . People are revengeful—do not mind them—do nothing but love me—if I knew that for certain life and health will in such event be a heaven, and death itself will be less painful. I long to believe in immortality I shall never to ab(le) to bid you an entire farewell. If I am destined to be happy with you here—how short is the longest Life—I wish to believe in immortality—I wish to live with you for ever. . . .

Letter from John Keats
to Fanny Brawne, June 1820.

Her Triumph

See the Chariot at hand here of Love,
   Wherein my Lady rideth!
Each that drawes, is a Swan, or a Dove,
   And well the Carre Love guideth.
As she goes, all hearts doe duty
               Unto her beauty;
And enamour'd, doe wish, so they might
               But enjoy such a sight,
That they still were to run by her side,
Thorough Swords, thorough Seas, whether she would ride.

Doe but looke on her eyes, they doe light
   All that Loves world compriseth!
Doe but looke on her Haire, it is bright
   As Loves starre when it riseth!
Doe but marke, her forehead's smoother
               Than words that sooth her!
And from her arched browes, such a grace
               Sheds it selfe through the face,
   As alone there triumphs to the life
All the Gaine, all the Good, of the Elements strife.

Have you seene but a bright Lillie grow,
   Before rude hands have touch'd it?
Ha' you mark'd but the fall o' the Snow
   Before the soyle hath smutch'd it?
Ha' you felt the wooll o' the Bever?
               Or Swans Downe ever?
Or have smelt o' the bud o' the Brier?
               Or the Nard in the fire?
   Or have tasted the bag of the Bee?
O so white! O so soft! O so sweet is she!

Ben Jonson

A Recollection

Famously she descended, her red hair
Unbound and bronzed by sea-reflections, caught
Crinkled with sea-pearls. The fine slender taut
Knees that let down her feet upon the air,

Young breasts, slim flanks and golden quarries were
Older than when the young distraught
Unknown Venetian, painting her portrait, thought
He'd not imagined what he painted there.

And I too commerced with that golden cloud:
Lipped her delicious hands and had my ease
Faring fantastically, perversely proud.

All loveliness demands our courtesies.
Since she was dead I praised her as I could
Silently, among the Barberini bees.

John Peale Bishop

St. Valentine's Day

To-day, all day, I rode upon the Down,
With hounds and horsemen, a brave company.
On this side in its glory lay the sea,
On that the Sussex Weald, a sea of brown.
The wind was light, and brightly the sun shone,
And still we galloped on from gorse to gorse.
And once, when checked, a thrush sang, and my horse

Pricked his quick ears as to a sound unknown.
I knew the Spring was come. I knew it even
Better than all by this, that through my chase
In bush and stone and hill and sea and heaven
I seemed to see and follow still your face.
Your face my quarry was. For it I rode,
My horse a thing of wings, myself a god.

Wilfrid Scawen Blunt

The Fair Singer

I

To make a final conquest of all me,
Love did compose so sweet an Enemy,
In whom both Beauties to my death agree,
Joyning themselves in fatal Harmony;
That while she with her Eyes my Heart does bind,
She with her Voice might captivate my Mind.

II

I could have fled from One but singly fair:
My dis-intangled Soul it self might save,
Breaking the curled trammels of her hair.
But how should I avoid to be her Slave,
Whose subtile Art invisibly can wreath
My Fetters of the very Air I breath?

III

It had been easie fighting in some plain,
Where Victory might hang in equal choice,
But all resistance against her is vain,

Who has th'advantage both of Eyes and Voice,
And all my Forces needs must be undone,
She having gained both the Wind and Sun.

Andrew Marvell

The Apostrophe to Vincentine

I

I figured you as nude between
Monotonous earth and dark blue sky.
It made you seem so small and lean
And nameless,
Heavenly Vincentine.

II

I saw you then, as warm as flesh,
Brunette,
But yet not too brunette,
As warm, as clean.
Your dress was green,
Was whited green,
Green Vincentine.

III

Then you came walking,
In a group
Of human others,
Voluble.
Yes: you came walking,
Vincentine.
Yes: you came talking.

IV

And what I knew you felt
Came then.
Monotonous earth I saw become
Illimitable spheres of you,
And that white animal, so lean,
Turned Vincentine,
Turned heavenly Vincentine,
And that white animal, so lean,
Turned heavenly, heavenly Vincentine.

Wallace Stevens

"Body of a woman, white hills, white thighs"

Body of a woman, white hills, white thighs,
When you surrender, you stretch out like the world.
My body, savage and peasant, undermines you
and makes a son leap in the bottom of the earth.

I was lonely as a tunnel. Birds flew from me.
And night invaded me with her powerful army.
To survive I forged you like a weapon,
like an arrow for my bow, or a stone for my sling.

But now the hour of revenge falls, and I love you.
Body of skin, of moss, of firm and thirsty milk!
And the cups of your breasts! And your eyes full of
    absence!
And the roses of your mound! And your voice slow and
    sad!

24

Body of my woman, I will live on through your
    marvelousness.
My thirst, my desire without end, my wavering road!
Dark river beds down which the eternal thirst is flowing,
and the fatigue is flowing, and the grief without shore.

Pablo Neruda
*Translated from the Spanish
by Robert Bly*

Sonnet: *A Rapture Concerning His Lady*

Who is she coming, whom all gaze upon,
Who makes the air all tremulous with light,
And at whose side is Love himself? that none
    Dare speak, but each man's sighs are infinite.
    Ah me! how she looks round from left to right,
Let Love discourse: I may not speak thereon.
Lady she seems of such high benison
    As makes all others graceless in men's sight.
The honour which is hers cannot be said;
    To whom are subject all things virtuous,
        While all things beauteous own her deity.
Ne'er was the mind of man so nobly led,
    Nor yet was such redemption granted us
        That we should ever know her perfectly.

Guido Cavalcanti
*Translated from the Italian
by Dante Gabriel Rossetti*

25

"With thee, in the Desert"

With thee, in the Desert—
With thee in the thirst—
With thee in the Tamarind wood—
Leopard breathes—at last!

Emily Dickinson

The Extasie

Where, like a pillow on a bed,
　A Pregnant banke swel'd up, to rest
The violets reclining head,
　Sat we two, one anothers best.
Our hands were firmely cimented
　With a fast balme, which thence did spring,
Our eye-beames twisted, and did thred
　Our eyes upon one double string;
So to'entergraft our hands, as yet
　Was all the meanes to make us one,
And pictures in our eyes to get
　Was all our propagation.
As 'twixt two equal Armies, Fate
　Suspends uncertaine victorie,
Our soules (which to advance their state,
　Were gone out,) hung 'twixt her, and mee.
And whil'st our soules negotiate there,
　Wee like sepulchrall statues lay;
All day, the same our postures were,
　And wee said nothing, all the day.

26

If any, so by love refin'd,
  That he soules language understood,
And by good love were growen all minde,
  Within convenient distance stood,
He (though he knew not which soule spake,
  Because both meant, both spake the same)
Might thence a new concoction take,
  And part farre purer then he came.
This Extasie doth unperplex
  (We said) and tell us what we love,
Wee see by this, it was not sexe,
  Wee see, we saw not what did move:
But as all severall soules containe
  Mixture of things, they know not what,
Love, these mixt soules doth mixe againe,
  And makes both one, each this and that.
A single violet transplant,
  The strength, the colour, and the size,
(All which before was poore, and scant,)
  Redoubles still, and multiplies.
When love, with one another so
  Interinanimates two soules,
That abler soule, which thence doth flow,
  Defects of lonelinesse controules.
Wee then, who are this new soule, know,
  Of what we are compos'd, and made,
For, th' Atomies of which we grow,
  Are soules, whom no change can invade.
But O alas, so long, so farre
  Our bodies why doe wee forbeare?
They are ours, though they'are not wee, Wee are
  The intelligences, they the spheare.
We owe them thankes, because they thus,
  Did us, to us, at first convay,
Yeelded their forces, sense, to us,
  Nor are drosse to us, but allay.

27

On man heavens influence workes not so,
  But that it first imprints the ayre,
Soe soule into the soule may flow,
  Though it to body first repaire.
As our blood labours to beget
  Spirits, as like soules as it can,
Because such fingers need to knit
  That subtile knot, which makes us man:
So must pure lovers soules descend
  T'affections, and to faculties,
Which sense may reach and apprehend,
  Else a great Prince in prison lies.
To'our bodies turne wee then, that so
  Weake men on love reveal'd may looke;
Loves mysteries in soules doe grow,
  But yet the body is his booke.
And if some lover, such as wee,
  Have heard this dialogue of one,
Let him still marke us, he shall see
  Small change, when we'are to bodies gone.

                                    John Donne

2

"Love, I note you, stroke by stroke,
And show you how you play
with shameless art . . ."

"Waking, I Always Waked You Awake"

Waking, I always waked you awake
As always I fell from the ledge of your arms
Into the soft sand and silt of sleep
Permitted by you awake, with your arms firm.

Waking, always I waked immediately
To the face you were when I was off sleeping,
Ribboned with sea weed or running with deer
In a valentine country of swans in the door.

Waking, always waked to the tasting of dew
As if my sleep issued tears for its loving
Waking, always waked, swimming from foam
Breathing from mountains clad in a cloud.

As waking, always waked in the health of your eyes,
Curled your leaf hair, uncovered your hands,
Good morning like birds in an innocence
Wild as the Indies we ever first found.

Jean Garrigue

"Wild Nights—Wild Nights!"

Wild Nights—Wild Nights!
Were I with thee
Wild Nights should be
Our luxury!

Futile—the Winds—
To a Heart in port—
Done with the Compass—
Done with the Chart!

Rowing in Eden—
Ah, the Sea!
Might I but moor—Tonight—
In Thee!

Emily Dickinson

Song: *"How sweet I roam'd*
    from field to field"

How sweet I roam'd from field to field,
    And tasted all the summer's pride,
'Till I the prince of love beheld,
    Who in the sunny beams did glide!

He shew'd me lilies for my hair,
    And blushing roses for my brow;
He led me through his gardens fair,
    Where all his golden pleasures grow.

With sweet May dews my wings were wet,
    And Phœbus fir'd by vocal rage;
He caught me in his silken net,
    And shut me in his golden cage.

He loves to sit and hear me sing,
    Then, laughing, sports and plays with me;
Then stretches out my golden wing,
    And mocks my loss of liberty.

                                William Blake

Dream-Pedlary

I

If there were dreams to sell,
    What would you buy?
Some cost a passing bell;
    Some a light sigh,
That shakes from Life's fresh crown
Only a roseleaf down.
If there were dreams to sell,
Merry and sad to tell,
And the crier rung the bell,
    What would you buy?

II

A cottage lone and still,
    With bowers nigh,
Shadowy, my woes to still,
    Until I die.
Such pearl from Life's fresh crown
Fain would I shake me down.
Were dreams to have at will,
This would best heal my ill,
    This would I buy.

III

But there were dreams to sell,
    Ill didst thou buy;
Life is a dream, they tell,
    Waking, to die.

Dreaming a dream to prize,
Is wishing ghosts to rise;
    And, if I had the spell
    To call the buried, well,
        Which one would I?

IV

If there are ghosts to raise,
    What shall I call,
Out of hell's murky haze,
    Heaven's blue hall?
Raise my loved longlost boy
To lead me to his joy.
    There are no ghosts to raise;
    Out of death lead no ways;
        Vain is the call.

V

Know'st thou not ghosts to sue?
    No love thou hast.
Else lie, as I will do,
    And breathe thy last.
So out of Life's fresh crown
Fall like a rose-leaf down.
    Thus are the ghosts to woo;
    Thus are all dreams made true,
        Ever to last!

Thomas Lovell Beddoes

"There came you wishing me ***"

There came you wishing me ***
And so I said ***
And then you turned your head
With the greatest beauty

Smiting me mercilessly!
And then you said ***
So that my heart was made
Into the strangest country . . .

*** you said, so beauteously,
So that an angel came
To hear that name,
And we caught him tremulously!

José Garcia Villa
*Translated from the Spanish
by Ben F. Carruthers*

Sapphics

All the night sleep came not upon my eyelids,
Shed not dew, nor shook nor unclosed a feather,
Yet with lips shut close and with eyes of iron
    Stood and beheld me.

Then to me so lying awake a vision
Came without sleep over the seas and touched me,
Softly touched mine eyelids and lips; and I too,
    Full of the vision,

36

Saw the white implacable Aphrodite,
Saw the hair unbound and the feet unsandalled
Shine as fire of sunset on western waters;
    Saw the reluctant

Feet, the straining plumes of the doves that drew her,
Looking always, looking with necks reverted,
Back to Lesbos, back to the hills whereunder
    Shone Mitylene;

Heard the flying feet of the Loves behind her
Make a sudden thunder upon the waters,
As the thunder flung from the strong unclosing
    Wings of a great wind.

So the goddess fled from her place, with awful
Sound of feet and thunder of wings around her;
While behind a clamour of singing women
    Severed the twilight.

Ah the singing, ah the delight, the passion!
All the Loves wept, listening; sick with anguish,
Stood the crowned nine Muses about Apollo;
    Fear was upon them,

While the tenth sang wonderful things they knew not.
Ah the tenth, the Lesbian! the nine were silent,
None endured the sound of her song for weeping;
    Laurel by laurel,

Faded all their crowns; but about her forehead,
Round her woven tresses and ashen temples
White as dead snow, paler than grass in summer,
    Ravaged with kisses,

Shone a light of fire as a crown for ever.
Yea, almost the implacable Aphrodite
Paused, and almost wept; such a song was that song.
    Yea, by her name too

Called her, saying, "Turn to me, O my Sappho";
Yet she turned her face from the Loves, she saw not
Tears for laughter darken immortal eyelids,
    Heard not about her

Fearful fitful wings of the doves departing,
Saw not how the bosom of Aphrodite
Shook with weeping, saw not her shaken raiment,
    Saw not her hands wrung;

Saw the Lesbians kissing across their smitten
Lutes with lips more sweet than the sound of lute-
        strings,
Mouth to mouth and hand upon hand, her chosen,
    Fairer than all men;

Only saw the beautiful lips and fingers,
Full of songs and kisses and little whispers,
Full of music; only beheld among them
    Soar, as a bird soars

Newly fledged, her visible song, a marvel,
Made of perfect sound and exceeding passion,
Sweetly shapen, terrible, full of thunders,
    Clothed with the wind's wings.

Then rejoiced she, laughing with love, and scattered
Roses, awful roses of holy blossom;
Then the Loves thronged sadly with hidden faces
    Round Aphrodite,

Then the Muses, stricken at heart, were silent;
Yea, the gods waxed pale; such a song was that song.
All reluctant, all with a fresh repulsion,
    Fled from before her.

All withdrew long since, and the land was barren,
Full of fruitless women and music only.
Now perchance, when winds are assuaged at sunset,
    Lulled at the dewfall,

By the grey sea-side, unassuaged, unheard of,
Unbeloved, unseen in the ebb of twilight,
Ghosts of outcast women return lamenting,
    Purged not in Lethe,

Clothed about with flame and with tears, and singing
Songs that move the heart of the shaken heaven,
Songs that break the heart of the earth with pity,
    Hearing, to hear them.

Algernon Charles Swinburne

La Bella Bona Roba

I

I cannot tell who loves the Skeleton
Of a poor Marmoset, nought but boan, boan.
Give me a nakedness with her cloath's on.

39

Such whose white-sattin upper coat of skin,
Cut upon Velvet rich Incarnadin,
Ha's yet a Body (and of Flesh) within.

III

Sure it is meant good Husbandry in men,
Who do incorporate with Aery leane,
T'repair their sides, and get their Ribb agen.

IV

Hard hap unto that Huntsman that Decrees
Fat joys for all his swet, when as he sees,
After his 'Say, nought but his Keepers Sees.

V

Then Love I beg, when next thou tak'st thy Bow,
Thy angry shafts, and dost Heart-chasing go,
Passe *Rascall Deare*, strike me the largest Doe.

John Wilmot, Earl of Rochester

In the Fields

Lord, when I look at lovely things which pass,
    Under old trees the shadows of young leaves
Dancing to please the wind along the grass,
    Or the gold stillness of the August sun on the August sheaves;
Can I believe there is a heavenlier world than this?

And if there is
Will the strange heart of any everlasting thing
    Bring me these dreams that take my breath away?
They come at evening with the home-flying rooks and the scent
      of hay,
    Over the fields. They come in Spring.

Charlotte Mew

Sonnet LXXV: *"One day I wrote her name upon the strand"*

One day I wrote her name upon the strand,
But came the waves and washed it away:
Agayne I wrote it with a second hand,
But came the tyde, and made my paynes his pray.
"Vayne man," sayd she, "that doest in vaine assay,
A mortall thing so to immortalize,
For I my selve shall lyke to this decay,
And eek my name bee wyped out lykewize."
"Not so," quod I, "let baser things devize
To dy in dust, but you shall live by fame:
My verse your vertues rare shall eternize,
And in the hevens wryte your glorious name.
Where whenas death shall all the world subdew,
Our love shall live, and later life renew."

Edmund Spenser

Inordinate Love

I shall say what inordinate love is:
The furiosite and wodness of minde,
A instinguible brenning fawting blis,
A gret hungre, insaciat to finde,
A dowcet ille, a ivell swetness blinde,
A right wonderfulle, sugred, swete errour,
Withoute labour rest, contrary to kinde,
Or withoute quiete to have huge labour.

John Lydgate

Gloire de Dijon

When she rises in the morning
I linger to watch her;
Spreads the bath-cloth underneath the window
And the sunbeams catch her
Glistening white on the shoulders,
While down her sides the mellow
Golden shadow glows as
She stoops to the sponge, and the swung breasts
Sway like full-blown yellow
Gloire de Dijon roses.

She drips herself with water, and the shoulders
Glisten as silver, they crumple up
Like wet and falling roses, and I listen
For the sluicing of their rain-dishevelled petals.

42

In the window full of sunlight
Concentrates her golden shadow
Fold on fold, until it glows as
Mellow as the glory roses.

D. H. Lawrence

A *Rapture*

I will enjoy thee now my *Celia*, come
   And flye with me to Loves Elizium:
The Gyant, Honour, that keepes cowards out,
Is but a Masquer, and the servile rout
Of baser subjects onely, bend in vaine
To the vast Idoll, whilst the nobler traine
Of valiant Lovers, daily sayle between
The huge Collosses legs, and passe unseene
Unto the blissfull shore; be bold, and wise,
And we shall enter, the grim Swisse denies
Only tame fooles a passage, that not know
He is but forme, and onely frights in show
The duller eyes that looke from farre; draw neere,
And thou shalt scorne, what we were wont to feare.
We shall see how the stalking Pageant goes
With borrowed legs, a heavie load to those
That made, and beare him; not as we once thought
The seeds of Gods, but a weake modell wrought
By greedy men, that seeke to enclose the common,
And within private armes empale free woman.
   Come then, and mounted on the wings of love
Wee'le cut the flitting ayre, and sore above
The Monsters head, and in the noblest seates
Of those blest shades, quench, and renew our heates.
There, shall the Queene of Love, and Innocence,
Beautie and Nature, banish all offence

From our close Ivy twines, there I'le behold
Thy bared snow, and thy unbraded gold.
There, my enfranchiz'd hand, on every side
Shall o're thy naked polish'd Ivory slide.
No curtaine there, though of transparent lawne
Shall be before thy virgin-treasure drawne;
But the rich Mine, to the enquiring eye
Expos'd, shall ready still for mintage lye,
And we will coyne young *Cupids*. There, a bed
Of Roses, and fresh Myrtles, shall be spread
Under the cooler shade of Cypresse groves:
Our pillowes, of the downe of *Venus* Doves,
Whereon our panting lims wee'le gently lay
In the faint respites of our active play;
That so our slumbers, may in dreames have leisure,
To tell the nimble fancie our past pleasure;
And so our soules that cannot be ambrac'd,
Shall the embraces of our bodyes taste.
Meane while the bubbling streame shall court the shore,
Th' enamoured chirping Wood-quire shall adore
In varied tunes the Deitie of Love;
The gentle blasts of Westerne winds, shall move
The trembling leaves, & through their close bows breath
Still Musick, whilst we rest our selves beneath
Their dancing shade; till a soft murmure, sent
From soules entranc'd in amorous languishment
Rowze us, and shoot into our veins fresh fire,
Till we, in their sweet extasie expire.
    Then, as the empty Bee, that lately bore,
Into the common treasure, all her store,
Flyes 'bout the painted field with nimble wing,
Defloering the fresh virgins of the Spring;
So will I rifle all the sweets, that dwell
In my delicious Paradise, and swell
My bagge with honey, drawne forth by the power
Of fervent kisses, from each spicie flower.
I'le seize the Rose-buds in their perfum'd bed,

44

The Violet knots, like curious Mazes spread
O're all the Garden, taste the ripned Cherry,
The warme, firme Apple, tipt with corall berry:
Then will I visit, with a wandring kisse,
The vale of Lillies, and the Bower of blisse:
And where the beauteous Region doth divide
Into two milkie wayes, my lips shall slide
Fowne those smooth Allies, wearing as I goe
A tract for lovers on the printed snow;
Thence climbing o're the swelling *Appenine*,
Retire into thy grove of Eglantine;
Where I will all those ravisht sweets distill
Through Loves Alimbique and with Chimmique skill
From the mixt masse, one soveraigne Balme derive,
Then bring that great *Elixar* to thy hive.
　Now in more subtile wreathes I will entwine
My sonowie thighes, my legs and armes with thine;
Thou like a sea of milke shalt lye display'd,
Whilst I the smooth, calme Ocean, invade
With such a tempest, as when *Jove* of old
Fell downe on *Danae* in a storme of gold:
Yet my tall Pine, shall in the *Cyprian* straight
Ride safe at Anchor, and unlade her fraight:
My Rudder, with thy bold hand, like a tryde
And skilfull Pilot, thou shalt steere, and guide
My Bark into Loves channell, where it shall
Dance, as the bounding waves doe rise or fall:
Then shall thy circling armes, embrace and clip
My willing bodie, and thy balmie lip
Bathe me in juyce of kisses, whose perfume
Like a religious incense shall consume
And send up holy vapours, to those powres
That blesse our loves, and crowne our sportfull houres,
That with such Halcion calmeness, fix our soules
In steadfast peace, as no affright controules.
There, no rude sounds shake us with sudden starts,
No jealous eares, when we unrip our hearts

Sucke our discourse in, no observing spies
This blush, that glance traduce; no envious eyes
Watch our close meetings, nor are we betray'd
To Rivals, by the bribed chamber-maid.
No wedlock bonds unwreathe our twisted loves;
We seeke no midnight Arbor, no darke groves
To hide our kisses, there, the hated name
Of husband, wife, lust, modest, chaste, or shame,
Are vaine and empty words, whose very sound
Was never heard in the Elizian ground.
All things are lawfull there, that may delight
Nature, or unrestrained Appetite;
Like, and enjoy, to will, and act, is one,
We only sinne when Loves rotes are not done.
     The Roman *Lucrece* there, reades the divine
Lectures of Loves great master, *Aretif,*
And knowes as well as *Lais,* how to move
Her plyant body in the act of love.
To quench the burning Ravisher, she hurles
Her limbs into a thousand winding curles,
And studies artfull postures, such as be
Carv'd on the barke of every neighbouring tree
By learned hands, that so adorn'd the rinde
Of those faire Plants, which as they lay entwinde,
Have fann'd their glowing fires. The Grecian Dame,
That in her endlesse webb, toyl'd for a name
As fruitless as her worke, doth there display
Her self before the Youth of *Ithaca,*
And th'amorous sport of gamesome nights prefer,
Before dull dreames of the lost Traveller.
Daphne hath broke her barke, and that swift foot,
Which th'angry Gods had fastned with a root
To the fixt earth, doth now unfetter'd run,
To meet th'embraces of the youthfull Sun:
She hangs upon him, like his Delphique Lyre,
Her kisses blow the old, and breath new fire:

Full of her God, she sings inspired Layes,
Sweet Odes of love, such as deserve the Bayes,
Which she her selfe was. Next her, *Laura* lyes
In *Petrarchs* learned armes, drying those eyes
That did in such sweet smooth-pac'd numbers flow,
As made the world enamour'd of his woe.
These, and ten thousand Beauties more, that dy'de
Slave to the Tyrant, now enlarg'd, deride
His cancell'd lawes, and for their time mispent,
Pay into Loves Exchequer double rent.
    Come then my *Celia*, wee'le no more forbeare
To taste our joyes, struck with a Pannique feare,
But will depose from his imperious sway
This proud *Userper* and walke free, as they
With necks unyoak's; nor is it just that Hee
Should fetter your soft sex with Chastitie,
Which Nature made unapt for abstinence;
When yet this false Impostor can dispence
With humane Justice, and with sacred right,
And maugre both their lawes command me fight
With Rivals, or with emulous Loves, that dare
Equall with thine, their Mistresse eyes, or haire:
If thou complaine of wrong, and call my sword
To carve out thy revenge, upon that word
He bids me fight and kill, or else he brands
With markes of infamie my coward hands,
And yet religion bids from blood-shed flye,
And damns me for that Act. Then tell me why
This Goblin Honour which the world adores,
Should make men Atheists, and not women Whores.

Thomas Carew

47

The Telephone

'When I was just as far as I could walk
From here today,
There was an hour
All still
When leaning with my head against a flower
I heard you talk.
Don't say I didn't, for I heard you say—
You spoke from that flower on the window sill—
Do you remember what it was you said?'

'First tell me what it was you thought you heard.'

'Having found the flower and driven a bee away,
I leaned my head,
And holding by the stalk,
I listened and I thought I caught the word—
What was it? Did you call me by my name?
Or did you say—
Someone said "Come"—I heard it as I bowed.'

'I may have thought as much, but not aloud.'

'Well, so I came.'

Robert Frost

48

Ode I, 23: *To Chloë*

You shun me, Chloë, wild and shy,
    As some stray fawn that seeks its mother
Through trackless woods. If spring winds sigh
    It vainly strives its fears to smother.

Its trembling knees assail each other
    When lizards stir the brambles dry;—
You shun me, Chloë, wild and shy,
    As some stray fawn that seeks its mother.

And yet no Libyan lion I,—
    No ravening thing to rend another;
Lay by your tears, your tremors dry,
    A husband's better than a brother;
Nor shun me, Chloë, wild and shy,
    As some stray fawn that seeks its mother.

Horace
*Translated from the Latin
by Austin Dobson*

Ode V: *"Not yet can she bear the yoke on submissive neck"*

Not yet can she bear the yoke on submissive neck,
not yet fulfil the duties of a mate, or endure the
vehemence of a lover. Upon the verdant meads
dwell the thoughts of thy love, who now allays the
oppressive heat amid the streams, and now is eager to
sport with her comrades in the moist willow-grove.

Away with desire for the unripe grape! Soon for
thee shall many-coloured Autumn paint the darken-
ing clusters purple. Soon shall she follow thee. For
Time courses madly on, and shall add to her the years
it takes from thee. Soon with eager forwardness shall
Lalage herself make quest of thee to be her mate,
beloved as was not shy Pholoë, nor Chloris, gleaming
with shoulder white, even as the unclouded moon
beams on midnight sea, nor Onidian Gyges, so fair that
should you put him in a band of maids, those who
knew him not would, for all their insight, fail to note
his difference from the rest, disguised by his flowing
locks and his girl-boy face.

Horace
*Translated from the Latin
by C. E. Bennett*

To a Friend

Well, Lizzie Anderson! seventeen men—and
the baby hard to find a father for!

What will the good Father in Heaven say
to the local judge if he do not solve this problem?
A little two-pointed smile and—pouff!—
the law is changed into a mouthful of phrases.

William Carlos Williams

"It may be"

It may be that a strange dream
Seized you tonight,
You thought you saw an angel
And it was your mirror.

In her flight Eléonore
Undid her long hair
To rob the dawn
Of the sweet object of my desire.

You should think no longer
Of some faithful husband.
I am the lover, I have wings
I will teach you to fly.

May the muse of falseness
Bring to the end of your fingers
That scorn which is but a dream
Of the shepherd prouder than a king.

Max Jacob
*Translated from the French
by Wallace Fowlie*

Her Words

A young mouth laughs at a gift.
She croons, like a cat to its claws;
Cries, 'I'm old enough to live
And delight in a lover's praise,
Yet keep to myself my own mind;
I dance to the right, to the left;
My luck raises the wind.'

'Write all my whispers down,'
She cries to her true love.
'I believe, I believe, in the moon!—
What weather of heaven is this?'

'The storm, the storm of a kiss.'

Theodore Roethke

3

"I loved you much
When everything had excellence at once . . ."

Dear Dark Head

Put your head, darling, darling, darling,
    Your darling black head my heart above;
Oh, mouth of honey with the thyme for fragrance,
    Who with heart in his breast could deny you love?

Oh, many and many a young girl for me is pining,
    Letting her locks of gold to the cold wind free,
For me, the foremost of our gay young fellows;
    But I'd leave a hundred, pure love, for thee!

Then put your head, darling, darling, darling,
    Your darling black head my heart above;
Oh, mouth of honey, with the thyme for fragrance,
    Who with heart in his breast could deny you love?

Anonymous
*Translated from the Gaelic
by Sir Samuel Ferguson*

The Basket-Weaver's Love

I loved you. I loved your face, like a wellspring
ravined by storms, and the secret of your domain enclosing
my caress. Some rely on a perfectly round imagination.
For me going is enough. I brought back from despair a basket
so small, my love, it could be woven of willow.

René Char
*Translated from the French
by Jackson Mathews*

Song: *"Give me leave to rail at you"*

Give me leave to rail at you,
I ask nothing but my due;
To call you false, and then to say
You shall not keep my heart a day:
But, alas! against my will,
I must be your captive still.
Ah! be kinder then: for I
Cannot change, and would not die.

Kindness has resistless charms,
All besides but weakly move,
Fiercest anger it disarms,
And clips the wings of flying love.
Beauty does the heart invade,
Kindness only can persuade;
It gilds the lover's servile chain,
And makes the slaves grow pleased again.

John Wilmot, Earl of Rochester

The One for All Time

If I say to you: "I have given up everything"
It means she is not the one of my body,
I never boasted of that,
It is not true
And the low fog where I move
Doesn't know whether I passed through.

The fan of her mouth, the reflection of her eyes,
I am the only one to speak of them,
I am the only one to be encircled
By this empty mirror where the air flows through me
And the air has a face, a beloved face,
A loving face, your face,
To you who have no name and whom other men do not know,
The sea says: on me, the sky says: on me,
The stars sense your presence, the clouds imagine you
And the blood spilled at the best moments,
The blood of generosity
Bears you with delight.

I sing the great joy of singing you,
The great joy of having you or not having you,
The candor of waiting for you, the innocence of knowing you,
You who efface forgetting, hope, ignorance,
Who efface absence and put me in the world,
I sing to sing, I love you for singing
The mystery where love creates me and frees itself.

You are pure, you are purer than I am.

Paul Eluard
*Translated from the French
by Wallace Fowlie*

Sonnet LXXVIII: *"Lackyng my loue I go from place to place"*

Lackyng my loue I go from place to place,
  lyke a young fawne that late hath lost the
    hynd:
  and seeke each where, where last I sawe her
    face,
  whose ymage yet I carry fresh in mynd.
I seeke the fields with her late footing synd,
  I seeke her bowre with her late presence deckt,
  yet nor in field nor bowre I her can fynd:
  yet field and bowre are full of her aspect.
But when myne eyes I thereunto direct,
  they ydly back returne to me agayne,
  and when I hope to see theyr trew obiect,
  I fynd my selfe but fed with fancies vayne.
Ceasse then myne eyes, to seeke her selfe to see,
  and let my thoughts behold her selfe in mee.

Edmund Spenser

The United States

The government of your body, sweet,
shall be my model for the world.
There is no desire in me to rule
that world or to advise it. Look
how it rouses with the sun, shuts
with night and sleeps fringed by
the slowly turning stars. I boil
I freeze before its tropics and its
cold. Its shocks are mine and to
the peaceful legislature of its seas,
by you its president,
I yield my willing services.

William Carlos Williams

To Earthward

Love at the lips was touch
As sweet as I could bear;
And once that seemed too much;
I lived on air

That crossed me from sweet things
The flow of—was it musk
From hidden grapevine springs
Down hill at dusk?

59

I had the swirl and ache
From sprays of honeysuckle
That when they're gathered shake
Dew on the knuckle.

I craved strong sweets, but those
Seemed strong when I was young;
The petal of the rose
It was that stung.

Now no joy but lacks salt
That is not dashed with pain
And weariness and fault;
I crave the stain

Of tears, the aftermark
Of almost too much love,
The sweet of bitter bark
And burning clove.

When stiff and sore and scarred
I take away my hand
From leaning on it hard
In grass and sand,

The hurt is not enough:
I long for weight and strength
To feel the earth as rough
To all my length.

Robert Frost

The Portrait

She speaks always in her own voice
Even to strangers; but those other women
Exercise their borrowed, or false, voices
Even on sons and daughters.

She can walk invisibly at noon
Along the high road; but those other women
Gleam phosphorescent—broad hips and gross fingers—
Down every lampless alley.

She is wild and innocent, pledged to love
Through all disaster; but those other women
Decry her for a witch or a common drab
And glare back when she greets them.

Here is her portrait, gazing sidelong at me,
The hair in disarray, the young eyes pleading:
'And you, love? As unlike those other men
As I those other women?'

Robert Graves

The Dalliance of the Eagles

Skirting the river road (my forenoon walk, my rest),
Skyward in air a sudden muffled sound, the dalliance of the
    eagles,
The rushing amorous contact high in space together,
The clinching, interlocking claws, a living, fierce, gyrating wheel,

Four beating wings, two beaks, a swirling mass tight grappling,
In tumbling, turning, clustering loops, straight downward falling,
Till o'er the river pois'd, the twain yet one, a moment's lull,
A motionless still balance in the air, then parting, talons loosing,
Upward again on slow-firm pinions slanting, their separate diverse
    flight,
She hers, he his, pursuing.

                                              Walt Whitman

A Song: *"Oh do not wanton with those eyes"*

Oh do not wanton with those eyes,
Lest I be sick with seeing;
Nor cast them down, but let them rise,
Lest shame destroy their being.
Oh be not angry with those fires,
For then their threats will kill me;
Nor look too kind on my desires,
For then my hopes will spill me.
Oh do not steep them in thy tears,
For so will sorrow slay me;
Nor spread them as distract with fears,
Mine own enough betray me.

                                              Ben Jonson

True Is True

"You say you love me truly,
But then how true is true?"
"How windy is the west wind,
How watery is dew?"

"I've heard the wind shift after dark,
And grass by noon is dry."
"How windy is the east wind?
At noon how high is high?"

"The faith of things is not the same.
They cannot ever err."
"Then my own mind must be a sleeping
Thing. It does not stir.

"It changes only when you do,
As winds go round and round."
She laughed, and taking both his hands
They circled without sound.

                                    Mark Van Doren

Étude

I hardly know you, and already I say to myself:
Will she never understand how her person exalts
all that there is in me of blood and fire?

As though it were much
to wait a few days—many? few?—
since all hope
seems a southern sea, deep, long!
And since we are always
fruits of impatience all forest.

I hardly know you and I have already demolished
cities clouds and landscapes journeys
and amazed, I discover suddenly

that I am within the actual stone
and that in the sky there are still no clouds.
How will these words be, new,
that now, when I am close to you, go flying forth
and show me in the accent of your hands
the ineffable limit of space.

Carlos Pellicer
*Translated from the Spanish
by H. R. Hays*

"Alter! When the Hills do"

Alter! When the Hills do—
Falter! When the Sun
Question if His Glory
Be the Perfect One—

Surfeit! When the Daffodil
Doth of the Dew—
Even as Herself—Sir—
I will—of You—

Emily Dickinson

To My Sister

It is the first mild day of March;
Each minute sweeter than before,
The redbreast sings from the tall larch
That stands beside our door.

There is a blessing in the air,
Which seems a sense of joy to yield
To the bare trees, and mountains bare,
And grass in the green field.

My sister! ('tis a wish of mine)
Now that our morning meal is done,
Make haste, your morning task resign;
Come forth and feel the sun.

Edward will come with you;—and, pray,
Put on with speed your woodland dress;
And bring no book; for this one day
We'll give to idleness.

No joyless forms shall regulate
Our living calendar;
We from to-day, my Friend, will date
The opening of the year.

Love, now a universal birth,
From heart to heart is stealing,
From earth to man, from man to earth:
—It is the hour of feeling.

One moment now may give us more
Than years of toiling reason:
Our minds shall drink at every pore
The spirit of the season.

Some silent laws our hearts will make,
Which they shall long obey:
We for the year to come may take
Our temper from to-day.

And from the blessed power that rolls
About, below, above,
We'll frame the measure of our souls:
They shall be tuned to love.

Then come, my Sister! come, I pray,
With speed put on your woodland dress;
And bring no book: for this one day
We'll give to idleness.

William Wordsworth

A Drinking Song

Wine comes in at the mouth
And love comes in at the eye;
That's all we shall know for truth
Before we grow old and die.
I lift the glass to my mouth,
I look at you, and I sigh.

W. B. Yeats

. . . I am certain I have not a right feeling towards Women—at this moment I am striving to be just to them but I cannot—Is it because they fall so far beneath my Boyish imagination? When I was a Schoolboy I though[t] a fair Woman a pure Goddess, my mind was a soft nest in which some one of them slept though she knew it not—I have no right to expect more than their reality. I thought them etherial above Men—I find then [*for* them] perhaps equal—great by comparison is very small—Insult may be inflicted in more ways than by Word or action—one who is tender of being insulted does not like to think an insult against another—I do not like to think insults in a Lady's Company—I commit a Crime with her which absence would have not known—Is it not extraordinary? When among Men I have no evil thoughts, no malice, no spleen—I feel free to speak or to be silent—I can listen and from every one I can learn—my hands are in my pockets I am free from all suspicion and comfortable. When I am among Women I have evil thoughts, malice spleen—I cannot speak or be silent—I am full of Suspicions and therefore listen to no thing—I am in a hurry to be gone—You must be charitable and put all this perversity to my being disappointed since Boyhood—Yet with such feelings I am happier alone among Crowds of men, by myself or with a friend or two—With all this trust me Bailey I have not the least idea that Men of different feelings and inclinations are more short sighted than myself—I never rejoiced more than at my Brother's Marriage and shall do so at that of any of my friends—. I must absolutely get over this—but how? The only way is to find the root of evil, and so cure it "with backward mutters of dissevering Power." That is a difficult thing; for an obstinate Prejudice can seldom be produced but from a gordian complication of feelings, which must take time to unravell and care to keep unravelled—I could say a good deal about this but I will leave it in hopes of better and more worthy dispositions . . .

Letter from John Keats
to Benjamin Bailey, 18–22 July 1818.

The Unfaithful Married Woman

I took her to the river,
Believing her unwed;
The fact she had a husband
Was something left unsaid.
St. James's night is timely—
She would not let me wait—
The lights are put out early,
The fireflies light up late.

I roused her sleeping bosom
Right early in our walk;
Her heart unfolded for me
Like hyacinths on the stalk.
Her starchy skirts kept rustling
And crackled in my ears
Like sheets of silk cut crosswise
At once by twenty shears.

The dark unsilvered treetops
Grew tall, as on we strode;
Dogs barked, a whole horizon,
Far from the river road.

When we had passed the brambles
And the thickets on our round,
Her coiled hair made a pillow
In a hollow on the ground;
As I undid my necktie,
Her petticoats left their place;
I shed my leather holster,
And she, four layers of lace.

68

Not nard nor snail had ever
Texture of skin so fine,
Nor crystal in the moonlight
Glimmered with purer shine:
Her thighs slipped from beneath me
Like little trout in fright,
Half chilly (but not frigid),
Half full of shining light.

The whole night saw me posting
Upon my lovely mare;
Mother-of-pearl the saddle,
No need for bridle and spur;
And what her whispers told me
A man should not repeat
When perfect understanding
Has made the mind discreet.

Dirty with sand and kisses
I brought her from the shore
As the iris poised green sabres
At the night wind once more.

To act in decent fashion
As loyal gypsy should,
I gave her a sewing-basket,
Satin and straw, and good;
And yet I would not love her
In spite of what she said
When I took her to the river,
For she was not unwed.

Federico García Lorca
Translated from the Spanish
by Rolfe Humphries

Parthenophil LXIII:
"Jove, for Europa's love took shape of bull"

Jove for Europa's love took shape of bull,
And for Calisto played Diana's part,
And in a golden shower he filled full
The laps of Danae, with celestial art.
Would I were changed but to my mistress' gloves,
That those white lovely fingers I might hide;
That I might kiss those hands which mine heart loves!
Or else that chain of pearl (her neck's vain pride)
Made proud with her neck's veins, that I might fold
About that lovely neck, and her paps tickle!
Or her to compass, like a belt of gold!
Or that sweet wine, which down her throat doth trickle,
To kiss her lips and lie next at her heart,
Run through her veins, and pass by pleasure's part!

Barnaby Barnes

70

Loves Deitie

I long to talke with some old lovers ghost,
   Who dyed before the god of Love was borne:
I cannot thinke that hee, who then lov'd most,
   Sunke so low, as to love one which did scorne.
But since this god produc'd a destinie,
And that vice-nature, custome, lets it be;
   I must love her, that loves not mee.

Sure, they which made him god, meant not so much,
   Nor he, in his young godhead practis'd it;
But when an even flame two hearts did touch,
   His office was indulgently to fit
Actives to passives. Correspondencie
Only his subject was; It cannot bee
   Love, till I love her, that loves mee.

But every moderne god will now extend
   His vast prerogative, as far as Jove.
To rage, to lust, to write to, to commend,
   All is the purlewe of the God of Love.
Oh were wee wak'ned by this Tyrannie
To ungod this child againe, it could not bee
   I should love her, who loves not mee.

Rebell and Atheist too, why murmure I,
   As though I felt the worst that love could doe?
Love might make me leave loving, or might trie
   A deeper plague, to make her love me too,
Which, since she loves before, I'am loth to see;
Falshood is worse than hate; and that must bee,
   If shee whom I love, should love mee.

John Donne

Spectral Lovers

By night they haunted a thicket of April mist,
Out of that black ground suddenly come to birth,
Else angels lost in each other and fallen on earth.
Lovers they knew they were, but why unclasped, unkissed?
Why should two lovers go frozen apart in fear?
And yet they were, they were.

Over the shredding of an April blossom
Scarcely her fingers touched him, quick with care,
Yet of evasions even she made a snare.
The heart was bold that clanged within her bosom,
The moment perfect, the time stopped for them,
Still her face turned from him.

Strong were the batteries of the April night
And the stealthy emanations of the field;
Should the walls of her prison undefended yield
And open her treasure to the first clamorous knight?
"This is the mad moon, and shall I surrender all?
If he but ask it I shall."

And gesturing largely to the moon of Easter,
Mincing his steps and swishing the jubilant grass,
Beheading some field-flowers that had come to pass,
He had reduced his tributaries faster
Had not considerations pinched his heart
Unfitly for his art.

"Am I reeling with the sap of April like a drunkard?
Blessed is he that taketh this richest of cities;
But it is so stainless the sack were a thousand pities.

This is that marble fortress not to be conquered,
Lest its white peace in the black flame turn to tinder
And an unutterable cinder."

They passed me once in April, in the mist.
No other season is it when one walks and discovers
Two tall and wandering, like spectral lovers,
White in the season's moon-gold and amethyst,
Who touch their quick fingers fluttering like a bird
Whose songs shall never be heard.

John Crowe Ransom

"What have I thus betrayed my libertie?"

What have I thus betrayed my libertie?
    Can those blacke beames such burning markes engrave
    In my free side? or am I borne a slave,
    Whose necke becomes such yoke of tyranny?

Or want I sense to feele my miserie?
    Or spirite, disdaine of such disdaine to have?
    Who for long faith, tho dayly helpe I crave,
    May get no almes but scorne of beggerie.

Vertue awake, Beautie but beautie is,
    I may, I must, I can, I will do
    Leave following that, which it is gaine to misse,

Let her go: soft, but here she comes, go to,
    Unkind, I love you not: O me, that eye
    Doth make my heart give to my tongue the lie.

Sir Philip Sidney

From MAUD: *"I have led her home, my love, my only friend"*

I have led her home, my love, my only friend.
There is none like her, none.
And never yet so warmly ran my blood
And sweetly, on and on,
Calming itself to the long-wish'd-for end,
Full to the banks, close on the promised good.

None like her, none.
Just now the dry-tongued laurels' pattering talk
Seem'd her light foot along the garden walk,
And shook my heart to think she comes once more;
But even then I heard her close the door,
The gates of Heaven are closed, and she is gone.

There is none like her, none,
Nor will be when our summers have deceased.
O, art thou sighing for Lebanon
In the long breeze that streams to thy delicious East,
Sighing for Lebanon,
Dark Cedar, tho' thy limbs have here increased
Upon a pastoral slope as fair,
And looking to the South, and fed
With honey'd rain and delicate air,
And haunted by the starry head
Of her whose gentle will has changed my fate,
And made my life a perfumed altar-flame;
And over whom thy darkness must have spread
With such delight as theirs of old, thy great
Forefathers of the thornless garden, there
Shadowing the snow-limb'd Eve from whom she came.

Alfred Tennyson

To His Mistresses

Helpe me! helpe me! now I call
To my pretty *Witchcrafts* all:
Old I am, and cannot do
That I was accustom'd to.
Bring your *Magicks*, *Spels*, and *Charmes*,
To enflesh my thighs, and armes:
Is there no way to beget
In my limbs their former heat?
Aeson had (as *Poets* faine)
Baths that made him young againe;
Find that *Medicine* (if you can)
For your drie-decrepid man:
Who would faine his strength renew,
Were it but to pleasure you.

Robert Herrick

Rhyme

What laid, I said,
My being waste?
'Twas your sweet flesh
With its sweet taste,—

Which, like a rose,
Fed with a breath,
And at its full
Belied all death.

75

It's at springs we drink;
It's bread we eat,
And no fine body,
Head to feet,

Shall force all bread
And drink together,
Nor be both sun
And hidden weather.

Ah no, it should not;
Let it be.
But once heart's feast
You were to me.

Louise Bogan

Clerk Saunders

Clerk Saunders and may Margret
   Walk'd owre yon garden green:
And sad and heavy was the love
   That fell thir twa between.

"A bed, a bed," Clerk Saunders said,
   "A bed for you and me."
"Fye na, fye na," said may Margret,
   "Till anes we married be.

"For in will come my seven brothers,
   And a' their torches burning bright;
They'll say, 'We have but one sister,
   And here her lying with a knight.' "

76

"Then I'll take the sword frae my scabbard
    And slowly slowly lift the pin;
And you may swear, and save your aith,
    Ye ne'er let Clerk Saunders in.

"Take you a napkin in your hand,
    And tie up baith your bonnie e'en,
And you may swear, and save your aith,
    Ye saw me na since late yestreen."

It was about the midnight hour
    When they asleep were laid,
When in and came her seven brothers,
    Wi' torches burning red:

When in and came her seven brothers,
    Wi' torches burning bright;
They said, "We hae but one sister,
    And behold her lying with a knight."

Then out and spake the first o' them,
    "I wot they have been lovers dear."
And out and spake the second o' them,
    "They have been in love this many a year."

Then out and spake the third o' them,
    "It were great sin true love to twain."
And out and spake the fourth o' them,
    "'Twere shame to slay a sleeping man."

Then out and spake the fifth o' them,
    "I wot they'll ne'er be twained by me."
And out and spake the sixth o' them,
    "We'll tak our leave and gae our way."

77

Then up and gat the seventh o' them,
    And never a word spake he;
But he has striped his bright brown brand
    Out through Clerk Saunders' fair bodye.

Clerk Saunders he started, and Margret she turn'd
    Into his arms as asleep she lay;
And sad and silent was the night
    That was atween these twae.

And they lay still, and sleepit sound,
    Until the day began to daw';
And kindly she to him did say,
    "It is time, true love, you were awa'."

But he lay still, and sleepit sound,
    Albeit the sun began to sheen;
She look'd atween her and the wa',
    And dull and drowsie were his e'en. . . .

Then in and came her father dear;
    Said, "Let a' your mourning be;
I'll carry the dead corse to the clay,
    And I'll come back and comfort thee."

"Comfort weel your seven sons,
    For comforted I will never be;
I ween 'twas neither knave nor loon
    Was in the bower last night wi' me."

The clinking bell gaed through the town,
    To carry the dead corse to the clay;
And Clerk Saunders stood at may Margret's window,
    I wot, an hour before the day.

"Are ye sleeping, Margret?" he says,
    "Or are ye waking presentlie?
Give me my faith and troth again,
    I wot, true love, I gied to thee."

"Your faith and troth ye sall never get,
    Nor our true love sall never twin,
Until ye come within my bower,
    And kiss me cheek and chin."

"My mouth it is full cold, Margret;
    It has the smell, now, of the ground;
And if I kiss thy comely mouth,
    Thy days of life will not be lang.

"O cocks are crowing a merry midnight;
    I wot the wild fowls are boding day;
Give me my faith and troth again,
    And let me fare me on my way."

"Thy faith and troth thou sallna get,
    And our true love shall never twin,
Until ye tell what comes o' women,
    I wot, who die in strong traivelling."

"Their beds are made in the heavens high,
    Down at the foot of our good Lord's knee,
Weel set about wi' gilly-flowers;
    I wot, sweet company for to see.

"O cocks are crowing a merry midnight;
    I wot the wild fowls are boding day;
The psalms of heaven will soon be sung,
    And I, ere now, will be miss'd away."

Then she has taken a crystal wand,
    And she has stroken her troth thereon;
She has given it him at the shot-window,
    Wi' mony a sad sigh and heavy groan.

"I thank ye, Margret; I thank ye, Margret;
    And ay I thank ye heartilie;
Gin ever the dead come for the quick,
    Be sure, Margret, I'll come for thee."

It's hosen and shoon, and gown alone,
    She climb'd the wall, and follow'd him,
Until she came to the green forest,
    And there she lost the sight o' him.

"Is there ony room at your head, Saunders?
    Is there ony room at your feet?
Or ony room at your side, Saunders,
    Where fain, fain, I wad sleep?"

"There's nae room at my head, Margret,
    There's nae room at my feet;
My bed it is fu' lowly now,
    Amang the hungry worms I sleep.

"Cauld mould is my covering now,
    But and my winding-sheet;
The dew it falls nae sooner down
    Than my resting-place is weet.

"But plait a wand o' bonny birk,
    And lay it on my breast;
And shed a tear upon my grave,
    And wish my saul gude rest."

Then up and crew the red, red cock,
    And up and crew the gray:
'Tis time, 'tis time, my dear Margret,
    That you were going away.

"And fair Margret, and rare Margret,
    And Margret o'veritie,
Gin e'er ye love another man,
    Ne'er love him as ye did me."

Anonymous

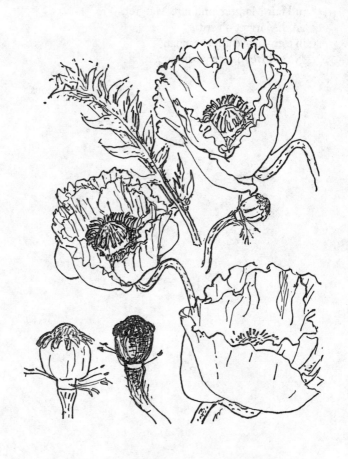

4

"And always in love we venture off some height
The nothing else can equal after it."

Upon the Intimations of Love's Mortality

It is the effort of the lie
Exacts a wounding pulse.
I loved you much
When everything had excellence at once.
First was our freshness and the stun of that.
Your body raved with music. What was lost
Is just that element our time always takes
And always in love we venture off some height
The nothing else can equal after it.
The thought of that bedevils me for miles.
How can I save you from my own despair
To think I may not love you as before?
Spoiled, we become accustomed to our luck.
This is the devil of the heart.
We were the smiles of gods awhile
And now, it seems, our ghosts must eat us up
Or wail in temples till our tombs are bought.
Attended now by shades of that great while,
Disguise is the nature of my guile
And yet the lie benumbs the soul.
Get me the purity of first sight!
Or strength to bear the after light.

Jean Garrigue

"Asleep! O sleep a little while, white pearl"

Asleep! O sleep a little while, white pearl!
And let me kneel, and let me pray to thee,
And let me call Heaven's blessing on thine eyes,
And let me breathe into the happy air,
That doth enfold and touch thee all about,
Vows of my slavery, my giving up,
My sudden adoration, my great love!

John Keats

Slumbersong

Some day, when I lose you,
will you be able to sleep without
my whispering myself away
like a linden's crown above you?

Without my waking here and laying down
words, almost like eyelids,
upon your breasts, upon your limbs,
upon your mouth?

Without my closing you and leaving
you alone with what is yours,
like a garden with a mass
of melissas and star-anise?

Rainer Maria Rilke
*Translated from the German
by M. D. Herter Norton*

86

"Always for the first time"

Always for the first time
I scarcely know you by sight
You come home at some hour of the night into a house oblique
    to my window
An imaginary house
It is there that from one moment to the next
In the complete dark
I wait until once more the fascinating ripping takes place
The one ripping
Of the façade of my heart
The closer I come to you
In reality
The more does the key sing in the door of the unknown room
Where you appear to me alone
You are first completely melted into the glittering
The fugitive angle of a curtain
In a field of jasmin I looked at at dawn on a road near Grasse
With its women fruit pickers diagonally
Behind them the dark falling wing of untrimmed seedlings
In front of them the square of the dazzling light
The invisibly raised curtain
In an uproar all the flowers come back
It is you at grips with the too long hour never troubled enough
    with sleep
You as if you could be
The same so close that I will perhaps never meet you
You pretend not to know I see you
Miraculously I am no longer sure you know it
Your idleness fills my eyes with tears
A cloud of interpretations surrounds each of your gestures
It is a honey-sweetened chase

87

There are rocking chairs on a bridge there are branches which
     might scratch you in the forest
In a shop window on rue Notre-Dame-de-Lorette there are
Two beautiful legs crossed wearing high stockings
Which open out in the center of a large white clock
There is a silk ladder unrolled over the ivy
There is
Hopeless fusion of your presence and your absence
I have found the secret
Of loving you
Always for the first time

                              André Breton
                              *Translated from the French
                              by Wallace Fowlie*

"Shall I come, sweet Love, to thee"

Shall I come, sweet Love, to thee,
     When the ev'ning beames are set?
Shall I not excluded be?
     Will you finde no fained lett?
Let me not, for pitty, more
Tell the long houres at your dore.

Who can tell what theefe or foe,
     In the covert of the night,
For his prey will worke my woe,
     Or through wicked foule despight:
So may I dye unredrest,
Ere my long love be possest.

But to let such dangers passe,
   Which a lovers thoughts disdaine,
'Tis enough in such a place
   To attend loves joyes in vaine.
Doe not mocke me in thy bed,
While these cold nights freeze me dead.

                  Thomas Campion

"I never saw you, madam, lay apart"

I never saw you, madam, lay apart
Your cornet black, in cold nor yet in heat,
Sith first ye knew of my desire so great
Which other fancies chased clean from my heart.
Whiles to myself I did the thought reserve
That so unware did wound my woeful breast,
Pity I saw within your heart did rest;
But since ye knew I did you love and serve
Your golden tress was clad alway in black,
Your smiling looks were hid thus evermore,
All that withdrawn that I did crave so sore.
So doth this cornet govern me, alack,
In summer sun, in winter breath of frost,
Of your fair eyes whereby the light is lost.

          Henry Howard, Earl of Surrey

The Mark

If, doubtful of your fate,
You seek to obliterate
And to forget
The counter-mark I set
In the warm blue-veined nook
Of your elbow crook,
How can you not repent
The experiment?

No knife nor fang went in
To lacerate the skin;
Nor may the eye
Tetter or wen descry:
The place which my lips pressed
Is coloured like the rest
And fed by the same blood
Of womanhood.

Acid, pumice-stone,
Lancings to the bone,
Would be in vain.
Here must the mark remain
As witness to such love
As nothing can remove
Or blur, or hide,
Save suicide.

Robert Graves

Love me little, love me long

You say, to me-wards your affection's strong;
Pray love me little, so you love me long.
Slowly goes farre: The meane is best: Desire
Grown violent, do's either die, or tire.

Robert Herrick

The Ballad of Villon and Fat Madge

' 'Tis no sin for a man to labour in his vocation.'
'The night cometh, when no man can work.'

What though the beauty I love and serve be cheap,
    Ought you to take me for a beast or fool?
All things a man could wish are in her keep;
    For her I turn swashbuckler in love's school.
    When folk drop in, I take my pot and stool
And fall to drinking with no more ado.
I fetch them bread, fruit, cheese, and water, too;
    I say all's right so long as I'm well paid;
'Look in again when your flesh troubles you,
    Inside this brothel where we drive our trade.'

But soon the devil's among us flesh and fell,
    When penniless to bed comes Madge my whore;
I loathe the very sight of her like hell.
    I snatch gown, girdle, surcoat, all she wore,
    And tell her, these shall stand against her score.

She grips her hips with both hands, cursing God,
Swearing by Jesus' body, bones, and blood,
   That they shall not. Then I, no whit dismayed,
Cross her cracked nose with some stray shiver of wood
   Inside this brothel where we drive our trade.

When all's up she drops me a windy word,
   Bloat like a beetle puffed and poisonous;
Grins, thumps my pate, and calls me dickey-bird,
   And cuffs me with a fist that's ponderous.
   We sleep like logs, being drunken both of us;
Then when we wake her womb begins to stir;
To save her seed she gets me under her
   Wheezing and whining, flat as planks are laid:
And thus she spoils me for a whoremonger
   Inside this brothel where we drive our trade.

Blow, hail or freeze, I've bread here baked rent free!
Whoring's my trade, and my whore pleases me;
   Bad cat, bad rat; we're just the same if weighed.
We that love filth, filth follows us, you see;
Honour flies from us, as from her we flee
   Inside this brothel where we drive our trade.

   I bequeath likewise to fat Madge
      This little song to learn and study;
   By God's head she's a sweet fad fadge,
      Devout and soft of flesh and ruddy;
   I love her with my soul and body,
   So doth she me, sweet dainty thing.
      If you fall in with such a lady,
   Read it, and give it her to sing.

François Villon
*Translated from the French
by Algernon Charles Swinburne*

Are You Born?—I

A man riding on the meaning of rivers
Sang to me from the cloud of the world:
Are you born? Are you born?
My name is gone into the burning heart
That knows the change deep in the form of things.
—I saw from the treeline all our cities shine.

A woman riding on the moon of ocean
Sang to me through the cloud of the world:
Are you born? Are you born?
The form of growing in leaf and crystal flows,
And in the eyes and rivers of the land.
—From the rock of our sky, I came to recognize.

A voice riding on the morning of air
Sang to me from the cloud of the world:
Are you born? Are you born?
Bring all the singing home;
There is a word of lightning in the grass.
—I stood alive in the young cloud.

                                        Muriel Rukeyser

Moon Compasses

I stole forth dimly in the dripping pause
Between two downpours to see what there was.
And a masked moon had spread down compass rays
To a cone mountain in the midnight haze,
As if the final estimate were hers,
And as it measured in her calipers,
The mountain stood exalted in its place.
So love will take between the hands a face. . . .

Robert Frost

Words for the Wind

1

Love, love, a lily's my care,
She's sweeter than a tree.
Loving, I use the air
Most lovingly: I breathe;
Mad in the wind I wear
Myself as I should be,
All's even with the odd,
My brother the vine is glad.

Are flower and seed the same?
What do the great dead say?
Sweet Phoebe, she's my theme:
She sways whenever I sway.
"O love me while I am,

94

You green thing in my way!"
I cried, and the birds came down
And made my song their own.

Motion can keep me still:
She kissed me out of thought
As a lovely substance will;
She wandered; I did not:
I stayed, and light fell
Across her pulsing throat;
I stared, and a garden stone
Slowly became the moon.

The shallow stream runs slack;
The wind creaks slowly by;
Out of a nestling's beak
Comes a tremulous cry
I cannot answer back;
A shape from deep in the eye—
That woman I saw in a stone—
Keeps pace when I walk alone.

2

The sun declares the earth;
The stones leap in the stream;
On a wide plain, beyond
The far stretch of a dream,
A field breaks like the sea;
The wind's white with her name,
And I walk with the wind.

The dove's my will today.
She sways, half in the sun:
Rose, easy on a stem,
One with the sighing vine,

One to be merry with,
And pleased to meet the moon.
She likes wherever I am.

Passion's enough to give
Shape to a random joy:
I cry delight: I know
The root, the core of a cry.
Swan-heart, arbutus-calm,
She moves when time is shy:
Love has a thing to do.

A fair thing grows more fair;
The green, the springing green
Makes an intenser day
Under the rising moon;
I smile, no mineral man;
I bear, but not alone,
The burden of this joy.

3

Under a southern wind,
The birds and fishes move
North, in a single stream;
The sharp stars swing around;
I get a step beyond
The wind, and there I am,
I'm odd and full of love.

Wisdom, where is it found?—
Those who embrace, believe.
Whatever was, still is,
Says a song tied to a tree.
Below, on the ferny ground,
In rivery air, at ease,
I walk with my true love.

96

What time's my heart? I care.
I cherish what I have
Had of the temporal:
I am no longer young
But the winds and waters are;
What falls away will fall;
All things bring me to love.

4

The breath of a long root,
The shy perimeter
Of the unfolding rose,
The green, the altered leaf,
The oyster's weeping foot,
And the incipient star—
Are part of what she is.
She wakes the ends of life.

Being myself, I sing
The soul's immediate joy.
Light, light, where's my repose?
A wind wreathes round a tree.
A thing is done: a thing
Body and spirit know
When I do what she does:
Creaturely creature, she!—

I kiss her moving mouth,
Her swart hilarious skin;
She breaks my breath in half;
She frolics like a beast;
And I dance round and round,
A fond and foolish man,
And see and suffer myself
In another being, at last.

Theodore Roethke

"I have not spent the April of my time"

I have not spent the April of my time,
The sweet of youth, in plotting in the air,
But do at first adventure seek to climb,
Whilst flowers of blooming years are green and fair.
I am no leaving of all-withering age,
I have not suffered many winter hours;
I feel no storm unless my love do rage,
And then in grief I spend both days and hours.
This yet doth comfort, that my flower lasted
Until it did approach my sun too near,
And then, alas, untimely was it blasted,
So soon as once thy beauty did appear.
But after all, my comfort rests in this,
That for thy sake my youth decayed is.

Bartholomew Griffin

. . . Notwithstand your Happiness and your recommendation I hope I shall never marry. Though the most beautiful Creature were waiting for me at the end of a Journey or a Walk; though the carpet were of Silk, the Curtains of the morning Clouds; the chairs and Sofa stuffed with Cygnet's down; the food Manna, the Wine beyond Claret, the Window opening on Winander mere, I should not feel—or rather my Happiness would not be so fine, as [*corrected from* and] my Solitude is sublime. Then instead of what I have described, there is a Sublimity to welcome me home—The roaring of the wind is my wife and the Stars through the window pane are my Children. The mighty abstract Idea I have of Beauty in all things stifles the more divided and minute domestic happiness—an amiable wife and sweet Children I contemplate as a part of that Bea(u)ty. but I must have a thousand of those beautiful particles to fill up my heart. I feel more and more every day, as my imagination strengthens, that I do not live in this world alone but in a thousand worlds—No sooner am I alone than shapes of epic greatness are stationed around me, and serve my Spirit the office of which is equivalent to a king's body guard—then 'Tragedy, with scepter'd pall, comes sweeping by' According to my state of mind I am with Achilles shouting in the Trenches or with Theocritus in the Vales of Sicily. Or I throw [*corrected from* through] my whole being into Triolus and repeating those lines, 'I wander, like a lost soul upon the stygian Banks staying for waftage,' I melt into the air with a voluptuousness so delicate that I am content to be alone—These things combined with the opinion I have of the generallity of women—who appear to me as children to whom I would rather give a Sugar Plum than my time, form a barrier against Matrimony which I rejoice in. . . .

Letter from John Keats
to the George Keatses, 14–31 *October* 1818.

A *Ballad upon a Wedding*

I tell thee, Dick, where I have been;
Where I the rarest things have seen,
    O, things without compare!
Such sights again cannot be found
In any place on English ground,
    Be it at wake or fair.

At Charing Cross, hard by the way
Where we, thou know'st, do sell our hay,
    There is a house with stairs;
And there did I see coming down
Such folks as are not in our town,
    Forty at least in pairs.

Amongst the rest one pest'lent fine,
His beard no bigger though than thine,
    Walked on before the rest:
Our landlord looks like nothing to him:
The King, God bless him!, 'twould undo him,
    Should he go still so dressed.

At Course-a-Park without all doubt
He should have first been taken out
    By all the maids i' th' town:
Though lusty Roger there had been,
Or little George upon the Green,
    Or Vincent of the Crown.

But wot you what? the youth was going
To make an end of all his wooing;
    The parson for him staid:
Yet by his leave, for all his haste,
He did not so much wish all past,
    Perchance, as did the maid.

The maid—and thereby hangs a tale;
For such a maid no Whitson-ale
    Could ever yet produce:
No grape, that's kindly ripe, could be
So round, so plump, so soft as she,
    Nor half so full of juice.

Her finger was so small, the ring
Would not stay on, which they did bring;
    It was too wide a peck:
And to say truth, for out it must,
It looked like the great collar, just,
    About our young colt's neck.

Her feet beneath her petticoat
Like little mice stole in and out,
    As if they feared the light:
But O, she dances such a way!
No sun upon an Easter-day
    Is half so fine a sight.

He would have kissed her once or twice;
But she would not, she was so nice,
    She would not do't in sight:
And then she looked as who should say,
"I will do what I list to-day,
    And you shall do't at night."

Her cheeks so rare a white was on,
No daisy makes comparison;
 Who sees them is undone:
For streaks of red were mingled there
Such as are on a Catherine pear,
 The side that's next the sun.

Her lips were red; and one was thin
Compared to that was next her chin,
 Some bee had stung it newly:
But, Dick, her eyes so guard her face
I durst no more upon them gaze
 Than on the sun in July.

Her mouth so small, when she does speak
Thou'dst swear her teeth her words did break
 That they might passage get;
But she so handled still the matter
They came as good as ours, or better,
 And are not spent a whit.

If wishing should be any sin,
The parson himself had guilty been,
 She looked that day so purely;
And, did the youth so oft the feat
At night, as some did in conceit,
 It would have spoiled him surely.

Just in the nick the cook knocked thrice,
And all the waiters in a trice
 His summons did obey:
Each serving-man, with dish in hand,
Marched boldly up, like our trained band,
 Presented, and away.

The business of the kitchen's great,
For it is fit that man should eat;
    Nor was it there denied—
Passion o' me, how I run on!
There's that that would be thought upon,
    I trow, besides the bride.

Now hats fly off and youths carouse,
Healths first go round and then the house:
    The bride's came thick and thick;
And, when 'twas named another's health,
Perhaps he made it hers by stealth;
    And who could help it, Dick?

O' th' sudden up they rise and dance;
Then sit again and sigh and glance;
    Then dance again and kiss:
Thus several ways the time did pass,
Whilst every woman wished her place,
    And every man wished his.

By this time all were stolen aside
To counsel and undress the bride;
    But that he must not know:
But yet 'twas thought he guessed her mind,
And did not mean to stay behind
    Above an hour or so.

When in he came, Dick, there she lay
Like new-fallen snow melting away;
    'Twas time, I trow, to part:
Kisses were now the only stay,
Which soon she gave, as one would say,
    Good-bye with all my heart.

But, just as Heavens would have, to cross it,
In came the bridesmaids with the posset;
    The bridegroom ate in spite:
For, had he left the women to't,
It would have cost two hours to do't,
    Which were too much that night.

At length the candle's out; and now
All that they had not done they do;
    What that is, who can tell?
But I believe it was no more
Than thou and I have done before
    With Bridget and with Nell.

Sir John Suckling

The Daisy

Having so rich a treasury, so fine a hoard
Of beauty water-bright before my eyes,
I plucked the daisy only, simple and white
In its fringed frock and brooch of innocent gold.

So is all equilibrium restored:
I leave the noontide wealth of richer bloom
To the destroyer, the impatient ravisher:
The intemperate bee, the immoderate bird.

Of all this beauty felt and seen and heard
I can be frugal and devout and plain,
Deprived so long of light and air and grass,
The shyest flower is sweetest to uncover.

How poor I was: and yet no richer lover
Discovered joy so deep in earth and water;
And in the air that fades from blue to pearl,
And in a flower white-frocked like my small daughter.

Marya Zaturenska

"Of all the Souls that stand create"

Of all the Souls that stand create—
I have elected—One—
When Sense from Spirit—flies away—
And Subterfuge—is done—
When that which is—and that which was—
Apart—intrinsic—stand—
And this brief Drama in the flesh—
Is shifted—like a Sand—
When Figures show their royal Front—
And Mists—are carved away,
Behold the Atom—I preferred—
To all the lists of Clay!

Emily Dickinson

"My sweetest Lesbia"

My sweetest Lesbia, let us live and love
And though the sager sort our deeds reprove,
Let us not weigh them. Heaven's great lamps do dive
Into their west, and straight again revive,
But, soon as once set is our little light,
Then must we sleep one ever-during night.

If all would lead their lives in love like me,
Then bloody swords and armor should not be;
No drum nor trumpet peaceful sleeps should move,
Unless alarm came from the camp of Love:
But fools do live and waste their little light,
And seek with pain their ever-during night.

When timely death my life and fortune ends,
Let not my hearse be vext with mourning friends,
But let all lovers rich in triumph come
And with sweet pastimes grace my happy tomb:
And, Lesbia, close up thou my little light,
And crown with love my ever-during night.

Catullus
Translated from the Latin
by Thomas Campion

Return

Return often and take me,
beloved sensation, return and take me—
when the memory of the body awakens,
and old desire again runs through the blood;
when the lips and the skin remember,
and the hands feel as if they touch again.

Return often and take me at night,
when the lips and the skin remember . . .

C. P. Cavafy
*Translated from the Greek
by Rae Dalven*

Love and Sleep

Lying asleep between the strokes of night
  I saw my love lean over my sad bed,
  Pale as the duskiest lily's leaf or head,
Smooth-skinned and dark, with bare throat made to bite,
Too wan for blushing and too warm for white,
  But perfect-coloured without white or red.
  And her lips opened amorously, and said—
I wist not what, saving one word—Delight.
And all her face was honey to my mouth,
  And all her body pasture to mine eyes;
    The long lithe arms and hotter hands than fire,
The quivering flanks, hair smelling of the south,
  The bright light feet, the splendid supple thighs
    And glittering eyelids of my soul's desire.

Algernon Charles Swinburne

The Dream

Me thought, (last night) love in an anger came,
And brought a rod, so whipt me with the same;
Mirtle the twigs were, meerly to imply;
Love strikes, but 'tis with gentle crueltie.
Patient I was; Love pitifull grew then,
And stroak'd the stripes, and I was whole agen.
Thus like a Bee, *Love-gentle* stil doth bring
Hony to salve, where he before did sting.

Robert Herrick

To Phillis to Love, and Live with Him

Live, live with me, and thou shalt see
The pleasures Ile prepare for thee:
What sweets the Country can afford
Shall blesse thy Bed, and blesse thy Board.
The soft sweet Mosse shall be thy bed,
With crawling Woodbine over-spread:
By which the silver-shedding streames
Shall gently melt thee into dreames.
Thy clothing next, shall be a Gowne
Made of the Fleeces purest Downe.
The tongues of Kids shall be thy meate;
Their Milke thy drinke; and thou shalt eate
The Paste of Filberts for thy bread
With Cream of Cowslips buttered:
Thy Feasting-Tables shall be Hills

With *Daisies* spread, and *Daffadils*;
Where thou shalt sit, and *Red-brest* by,
For meat, shall give thee melody.
Ile give thee Chaines and Carkanets
Of *Primroses* and *Violets*.
A Bag and Bottle thou shalt have;
That richly wrought, and This as brave;
So that as either shall expresse
The Wearer's no meane Shepheardesse.
At Sheering-times, and yearely Wakes,
When *Themilis* his pastime makes,
There thou shalt be; and be the wit,
Nay more, the Feast, and grace of it.
On Holy-dayes, when Virgins meet
To dance the Heyes with nimble feet;
Thou shalt come forth, and then appeare
The *Queen of Roses* for that yeere.
And having danc't ('bove all the best)
Carry the Garland from the rest.
In Wicker-baskets Maids shal bring
To thee (my dearest Shephardling)
The blushing Apple, bashfull Peare,
And shame-fac't Plum, (all simp'ring there).
Walk in the Groves, and thou shalt find
The name of *Phillis* in the Rind
Of every straight, and smooth-skin tree;
Where kissing that, Ile twice kisse thee.
To thee, a Sheep-hook I will send,
Be-pranckt with Ribbands, to this end,
This, this alluring Hook might be
Lesse for to catch a sheep, then me.
Thou shalt have Possets, Wassails fine,
Not made of Ale, but spiced Wine;
To make thy Maids and selfe free mirth,
All sitting neer the glitt'ring Hearth.
Thou sha't have Ribbands, Roses, Rings,

Gloves, Garters, Stockings, Shooes, and Strings
Of winning Colours, that shall move
Others to Lust, but me to Love.
These (nay) and more, thine own shal be,
If thou wilt love, and live with me.

Robert Herrick

Wedding-Wind

The wind blew all my wedding-day,
And my wedding-night was the night of the high wind;
And a stable door was banging, again and again,
That he must go and shut it, leaving me
Stupid in candlelight, hearing rain,
Seeing my face in the twisted candlestick,
Yet seeing nothing. When he came back
He said the horses were restless, and I was sad
That any man or beast that night should lack
The happiness I had.

Now in the day
All's ravelled under the sun by the wind's blowing.
He has gone to look at the floods, and I
Carry a chipped pail to the chicken-run,
Set it down, and stare. All is the wind
Hunting through clouds and forests, thrashing
My apron and the hanging cloths on the line.
Can it be borne, this bodying-forth by wind
Of joy my actions turn on, like a thread
Carrying beads? Shall I be let to sleep

Now this perpetual morning shares my bed?
Can even death dry up
These new delighted lakes, conclude
Our kneeling as cattle by all-generous waters?

Philip Larkin

"There came a Day at Summer's full"

There came a Day at Summer's full,
Entirely for me—
I thought that such were for the Saints,
Where Resurrections—be—

The Sun, as common, went abroad,
The flowers, accustomed, blew,
As if no soul the solstice passed
That maketh all things new—

The time was scarce profaned, by speech—
The symbol of a word
Was needless, as at Sacrament,
The Wardrobe—of our Lord—

Each was to each The Sealed Church,
Permitted to commune this—time—
Lest we too awkward show
At Supper of the Lamb.

The Hours slid fast—as Hours will,
Clutched tight, by greedy hands—
So faces on two Decks, look back
Bound to opposing lands—

And so when all the time had leaked,
Without external sound
Each bound the Other's Crucifix—
We gave no other Bond—

Sufficient troth, that we shall rise—
Deposed—at length, the Grave—
To that new Marriage,
Justified—through Calvaries of Love—

Emily Dickinson

La Belle Dame Sans Merci

O what can ail thee, knight-at-arms,
　　Alone and palely loitering?
The sedge has withered from the lake,
　　And no birds sing.

O what can ail thee, knight-at-arms,
　　So haggard and so woe-begone?
The squirrel's granary is full,
　　And the harvest's done.

I see a lily on thy brow
　　With anguish moist and fever dew,
And on thy cheeks a fading rose
　　Fast withereth too.

I met a lady in the meads,
　　Full beautiful—a faery's child,
Her hair was long, her foot was light,
　　And her eyes were wild.

I made a garland for her head,
    And bracelets too, and fragrant zone,
She looked at me as she did love,
    And made sweet moan.

I set her on my pacing steed,
    And nothing else saw all day long.
For sidelong would she bend, and sing
    A faery's song.

She found me roots of relish sweet,
    And honey wild, and manna dew,
And sure in language strange she said—
    "I love thee true!"

She took me to her elfin grot,
    And there she wept and sighed full sore,
And there I shut her wild, wild eyes
    With kisses four.

And there she lulléd me asleep,
    And there I dreamed—ah, woe betide!
The latest dream I ever dreamed
    On the cold hill side.

I saw pale kings and princes too,
    Pale warriors, death-pale were they all;
They cried—"La Belle Dame sans Merci
    Hath thee in thrall!"

I saw their starved lips in the gloam,
    With horrid warning gapéd wide,
And I awoke and found me here,
    On the cold hill's side.

And this is why I sojourn here,
  Alone and palely loitering,
Though the sedge is withered from the lake,
  And no birds sing.

John Keats

5

"Love is the sternest master of the school."

Last Letter to the Scholar

Come, lecturer on love, resume your rostrum.
Preach to the mad dead roses of the year.
Preach to my heart that's buried in the garden
Under the yellowed petals since you left.
Though deaf by those haranguing winds
The winter plagues dead petals with, and leaves
Long fluttering upon the barren ground or straying
Around the broken stems and shackled thorns,
Your voice by its compelling sweetness will
Spring to winter bring, and numb roots start
Alive to pierce and quick the dark
That closed around with killing cold what heart
I had, after you'd come and left.

My dear, you'll call this fallacy
Pretentious, or some fustian idiocy
To claim my ticking heart was put from me
Into some troped-up garden of old rue.
Forgive, because I set up roses too,
Improbable as madrigals. And chide
My errant language that would claim
I died, or nearly died, for loss of you.
Chide, but believe. I live, but I am dead.
But that's not what I mean. Who lives
Must learn to live his deaths. Who loves
Must learn the same. We blaze and char
As love is near or far
In that small world that's ordered to our want
But likewise bounded by love's eyes and lips.

The expanded world thus so contracted, what
Fires that come consume us when they're out.
And death's more amorous than not
And just as subtle sudden and chameleon cruel.

So preach to me, and tell me less of death
Than love that outlasts death, as I've heard tell.
Tell me that my heart confined
And sunken low within the flesh's earth
Will, when you come again, awake
And know its Easter in your sight
As may those thwarted roses rise
Some later on to your rare light
Compounded of much heat and spirit.
Tell me that this death's not long.
Be hortatory, admonitory, and calm
In your bright fever, that the clear estate
The world is when you're here will get again
Its lease to be, as you propound
How to our destiny we grow as one
If two, with such split hearts as we own,
Not sanguined by experience, may so dream
An absolution clement as the rain.

                                        Jean Garrigue

"When I was one-and-twenty"

When I was one-and-twenty
  I heard a wise man say,
"Give crowns and pounds and guineas
  But not your heart away;
Give pearls away and rubies
  But keep your fancy free."
But I was one-and-twenty,
  No use to talk to me.

When I was one-and-twenty
  I heard him say again,
"The heart out of the bosom
  Was never given in vain;
'Tis paid with sighs a-plenty
  And sold for endless rue."
And I am two-and-twenty,
  And oh, 'tis true, 'tis true.

A. E. Housman

"Alas, madam, for stealing of a kiss"

Alas, madam, for stealing of a kiss,
  Have I so much your mind then offended?
Have I then done so grievously amiss,
  That by no means it may be amended?
Then revenge you, and the next way is this:
  Another kiss shall have my life ended.
For to my mouth the first my heart did suck,
The next shall clean out of my breast it pluck.

Sir Thomas Wyatt

Morning

Look, my love, on the wall, and here, at this Eastern picture.
How still its scene, and neither of sleep nor waking:
No shadow falls from the tree or the golden mountain,
The boats on the glassy lake have no reflection,
No echo would come if you blew a horn in those valleys.

And look away, and move. Or speak, or sing:
And voices of the past murmur among your words,
Under your glance my dead selves quicken and stir,
And a thousand shadows attend you where you go.

That is your movement. There is a golden stillness,
Soundless and fathomless, and far beyond it;
When brow on brow, or mouth to mouth assembled,
We lie in the calm of morning. And there, outside us,
The sun moves on, the boat jogs on the lake,
The huntsman calls.
And we lie here, our orient peace awaking
No echo, and no shadow, and no reflection.

Henry Reed

The Excuse

Calling to mind, mine eye long went about
T' entice my heart to seek to leave my breast,
All in a rage I thought to pull it out,
By whose device I lived in such unrest.
    What could it say to purchase so my grace?
    Forsooth, that it had seen my mistress' face.

Another time, I likewise call to mind,
My heart was he that all my woe had wrought,
For he my breast the fort of love resigned,
When of such wars my fancy never thought.
    What could it say when I would him have slain?
    But he was yours, and had forgone me clean.

At length, when I perceived both eye and heart
Excused themselves as guiltless of mine ill,
I found myself was cause of all my smart,
And told myself, myself now slay I will;
    But when I found my self to you was true,
    I loved myself, because myself loved you.

Sir Walter Raleigh

"Never give all the heart"

Never give all the heart, for love
Will hardly seem worth thinking of
To passionate women if it seem
Certain, and they never dream
That it fades out from kiss to kiss;
For everything that's lovely is
But a brief, dreamy, kind delight.
O never give the heart outright,
For they, for all smooth lips can say,
Have given their hearts up to the play.
And who could play it well enough
If deaf and dumb and blind with love?
He that made this knows all the cost,
For he gave all his heart and lost.

W. B. Yeats

The Footsteps

Born of my voiceless time, your steps
Slowly, ecstatically advance:
Toward my expectation's bed
They move in a hushed, ice-clear trance.

Pure being, shadow-shape divine—
Your step deliberate, how sweet!
God!—every gift I have imagined
Comes to me on those naked feet.

If so it be your offered mouth
Is shaped already to appease
That which occupied my thought
With the live substance of a kiss,

Oh hasten not this loving act,
Rapture where self and not-self meet:
My life has been the awaiting you,
Your footfall was my own heart's beat.

Paul Valéry
*Translated from the French
by C. Day Lewis*

The Apparition

My pillow won't tell me
    Where he has gone,
The soft-footed one
    Who passed by, alone.

Who took my heart, whole,
    With a tilt of his eye,
And with it, my soul,
    And it like to die.

I twist and I turn,
    My breath but a sigh.
Dare I grieve? Dare I mourn?
    He walks by. He walks by.

Theodore Roethke

The Pearl

There is a myth, a tale men tell:
Each mussel shell
That in the ocean's bitter deep doth lie,
When it has wrought its pearl, must straightway die.
O Love, thou art the pearl my heart hath made,
And I am sore afraid.

Hans Christian Andersen
*Translated from the Danish
by Charles Wharton Stork*

124

The Mask

Always when I write I wear a mask,
A long antique Venetian mask
With a low forehead,
Like a great white satin snout.
I sit at the table and lift my head,
Gazing at myself in the glass, full-face
And then at an angle, beholding
The childish, bestial profile that I love.
Oh, if only a reader, the brother whom I address
Across this pallid, glittering mask,
Would come to plant a slow, heavy kiss
On this low forehead and wan cheek,
And bring to my face the full weight
Of that other, hollow and perfumed like mine!

Valery Larbaud
*Translated from the French
by William Jay Smith*

Aire and Angels

Twice or thrice had I loved thee,
Before I knew thy face or name,
So in a voice, so in a shapelesse flame,
Angells affect us oft, and worship'd bee;
    Still when, to where thou wert, I came,
Some lovely glorious nothing I did see.
    But since my soule, whose child love is,

Takes limmes of flesh, and else could nothing doe,
    More subtile than the parent is,
Love must not be, but take a body too,
    And therefore what thou wert, and who,
        I bid Love aske, and now
That it assume thy body, I allow,
And fixe it selfe in thy lip, eye and brow.

Whilst thus to ballast love, I thought,
And so more steddily to have gone,
With wares which would sinke admiration,
I saw, I had loves pinnace overfraught,
    Ev'ry thy haire for love to worke upon
Is much too much, some fitter must be sought;
    For, nor in nothing, nor in things
Extreme, and scatt'ring bright, can love inhere;
    Then as an Angell, face and wings
Of aire, not pure as it, yet pure doth weare,
    So thy love may be my loves spheare;
        Just such disparitie
As is twixt Aire and Angells puritie,
'Twixt womens love, and mens will ever bee.

John Donne

She

She stepped two paces forward
And two paces back
The first step said good morning sir
The second step said good morning ma'am
And the others said how is your family
Today is as lovely a day as a dove in the sky
She was wearing a burning shirt

Her eyes were sea-lulling
She had hidden a dream in a dark closet
She had met a dead man in the middle of her head
When she arrived she would leave a lovelier part far away
When she left something would take shape to wait for her on
  the horizon
Her glances were wounded and bled upon the hill
Her breasts were wide and she sang the dusks of her age
She was lovely as the sky beneath a dove
Her mouth was steel
And a deathbound banner was traced between her lips
She would laugh like the sea that feels coals in its belly
Like the sea when the moon watches itself drown
Like the sea that has bitten at all the beaches
The sea overflowing and falling into the void in times of
  abundance
When the stars coo above our heads
Before the north wind opens its eyes
She was lovely in her horizons of bones
With her burning shirt and her weary tree eyes
Like the sky on horseback above the doves

Vicente Huidobro
*Translated from the Spanish
by Dudley Fitts*

The Little Old Women

Les Petites vieilles

To Victor Hugo

In the winding folds of old capitals,
Where horror itself turns to enchantment,
Following my fatal moods, I spy on
Certain beings, decrepit and charming,

127

Misshapen creatures, these were once women,
Eponine or Lais! Broken or humped,
Or twisted, let us love them! they are souls.
Whipped by iniquitous north-winds they creep

In their tattered skirts and chilly fabrics,
Shaken by the din of omnibuses,
Clasping to their sides like relics tiny
Bags embroidered with flowers or rebuses;

They toddle like little marionettes,
Or drag their bodies like hurt animals,
Or dance without wishing to dance, poor bells
Swung by a pitiless demon! Broken

As they are, they have eyes that pierce like drills
And glimmer like the holes where water sleeps
At night; the divine eyes of little girls,
Who laugh with amazement at shiny things.

Have you noticed how the coffins of old
Women are often as small as a child's?
Canny Death in these like biers evinces
A bizarre and captivating taste,

And whenever I see one of these ghosts
Threading the teeming tableau of Paris,
It seems to me that the fragile creature
Is going softly towards a new cradle;

Unless, meditating on geometry,
I conjecture from the discordant limbs
How many times the workman must vary
The shape of the box that will hold these forms.

—Their eyes are ponds made of a million tears,
Crucibles spangled with a cooled metal . . .
Mysterious eyes, invincibly charming
To one suckled by austere misfortune!

Ah how many of them I have followed!
And one, at the hour when the sinking sun
Bloodies the sky with vermillion wounds,
Sat thoughtfully by herself on a bench

To hear one of those concerts rich with brass
With which the soldiers sometimes flood our parks,
Pouring on golden evenings a kind of
Heroism in the hearts of burgesses.

She, still straight, proud, and feeling the rhythm,
Drank in avidly the bright, warlike song,
Her eye opening like an old eagle's,
And her brow as if made for the laurel!

You go your way, stoic and uncomplaining,
Threading the chaos of living cities,
Mothers of the bleeding heart, courtesans
Or saints, whose names were once on every tongue.

You who were all of grace or all of glory,
None recognizes you! A rude drunkard
Mocks you in passing with a show of love;
A wretched child runs skipping at your heels.

Ashamed to be alive, shrunken shadows,
Fearful, with bent backs you hug the walls;
And no one speaks to you, strangely destined!
Human debris ripe for eternity!

But I, who watch tenderly, anxiously
At a distance your uncertain footsteps,
As if I were your father, what marvel!
Without your knowledge, taste clandestine pleasures:

I watch your novice passions unfolding;
Dark or bright, I summon up your lost days;
My heart, multiplied, revels in your vices!
My soul grows resplendent with your virtues!

O ruins! congeneric brains! each night I
Take solemn adieu of you! Where will you be
Tomorrow, octogenarian Eves,
On whom the dreadful claw of God lies heavy?

> Charles Baudelaire
> *Translated from the French*
> *by Barbara Gibbs*

"My true Love hath my heart, and I have his"

My true Love hath my heart, and I have his,
By just exchange one for the other given:
I hold his dear, and mine he cannot miss;
There never was a better bargain driven.
His heart in me keeps me and him in one,
My heart in him his thoughts and senses guides:
He loves my heart, for once it was his own;
I cherish his because in me it bides.
His heart his wound receivëd from my sight,
My heart was wounded with his wounded heart;
For as from me, on him his hurt did light,
So still methought in me his hurt did smart.
  Both, equal hurt, in this change sought our bliss:
  My true Love hath my heart, and I have his.

> Sir Philip Sidney

The Rigs o' Barley

It was upon a Lammas night,
    When corn rigs are bonie,
Beneath the moon's unclouded light,
    I held awa to Annie;
The time flew by, wi' tentless heed,
    Till, 'tween the late and early,
Wi' sma' persuasion she agreed
    To see me thro' the barley.

Corn rigs, an' barley rigs,
    An' corn rigs are bonie:
I'll ne'er forget that happy night
    Amang the rigs wi' Annie.

The sky was blue, the wind was still,
    The moon was shining clearly;
I set her down, wi' right good will,
    Amang the rigs o' barley:
I ken't her heart was a' my ain;
    I lov'd her most sincerely;
I kiss'd her owre and owre again,
    Amang the rigs o' barley.
        Corn rigs, an' barley rigs, etc.

I lock'd her in my fond embrace;
    Her heart was beating rarely:
My blessings on that happy place,
    Amang the rigs o' barley!
But by the moon and stars so bright,
    That shone that hour so clearly!
She aye shall bless that happy night
    Amang the rigs o' barley.
        Corn rigs, an' barley rigs, etc.

I hae been blythe wi' comrades dear;
  I hae been merry drinking;
I hae been joyfu' gath'rin gear;
  I hae been happy thinking;
But a' the pleasures e'er I saw,
  Tho' three times doubl'd fairly,
That night was worth them a'
  Amang the rigs o' barley.
            Corn rigs, an' barley rigs, etc.

                                    Robert Burns

"I leave this at your ear"

(For Nessie Dunsmuir)

I leave this at your ear for when you wake,
A creature in its abstract cage asleep.
Your dreams blindfold you by the light they make.

The owl called from the naked-woman tree
As I came down by the Kyle farm to hear
Your house silent by the speaking sea.

I have come late but I have come before
Later with slaked steps from stone to stone
To hope to find you listening for the door.

I stand in the ticking room. My dear, I take
A moth kiss from your breath. The shore gulls cry.
I leave this at your ear for when you wake.

                                    W. S. Graham

132

Roman Candle

It bursts and holds
a glittering gown for a ghost
but drifts and fades as we sigh
and exclaim, bursts again, and again.
Now what sparkles fall on grass,
whisper in pools, what poem
twinkles eternity, then cools?

All in a moment made is melting,
made by a hammer's quick bliss,
and we depart, lie down by fountains,
kiss. Quick, dear stain,
take the high and wed,
bury in the sky
before dark fades you again.

                                        Neil Weiss

"if i have made, my lady, intricate"

if i have made, my lady, intricate
imperfect various things chiefly which wrong
your eyes (frailer than most deep dreams are frail)
songs less firm than your body's whitest song
upon my mind—if i have failed to snare
the glance too shy—if through my singing slips
the very skillful strangeness of your smile
the keen primeval silence of your hair

—let the world say "his most wise music stole
nothing from death"—

                  you only will create
(who are so perfectly alive) my shame:
lady through whose profound and fragile lips
the sweet small clumsy feet of April came

into the ragged meadow of my soul.

                           E. E. Cummings

Lovesong

How shall I withhold my soul so that
it does not touch on yours? How shall I
uplift it over you to other things?
Ah willingly would I by some
lost thing in the dark give it harbor
in an unfamiliar silent place
that does not vibrate on when your depths vibrate.
Yet everything that touches us, you and me,
takes us together as a bow's stroke does,
that out of two strings draws a single voice.
Upon what instrument are we two spanned?
And what player has us in his hand?
O sweet song.

                    Rainer Maria Rilke
                    Translated from the German
                    by M. D. Herter Norton

A *Calvinist in Love*

I will not kiss you, country fashion,
    By hedgesides where
    Weasel and hare
Claim kinship with our passion.

I care no more for fickle moonlight:
    Would rather see
    Your face touch me
Under a claywork dune-light.

I want no scent or softness round us
    When we embrace:
    We could not trace
Therein what beauties bound us.

This bare clay-pit is truest setting
    For love like ours:
    No bed of flowers,
But sand-ledge for our petting.

The Spring is not our mating season:
    The lift of sap
    Would but entrap
Our souls and lead to treason.

This truculent gale, this pang of winter
    Awake our joy,
    For they employ
Moods that made Calvary splinter.

We need no vague and dreamy fancies:
    Care not to sight
    The Infinite
In transient necromancies.

No poetry on earth can fasten
    Its vampire mouth
    Upon our youth:
We know the sly assassin.

We cannot fuse with fallen Nature's
    Our rhythmic tide:
    It is allied
With laws beyond the creatures.

It draws from older, sterner oceans
    Its sensuous swell:
    Too near to Hell
Are we for earthly motions.

Our love is full-grown Dogma's offspring,
    Election's child,
    Making the wild
Heats of our blood an offering.

                        Jack Clemo

Socrates and Alcibiades

'Holy Socrates, why always with deference
  Do you treat this young man? Don't you know greater things?
    Why so lovingly, raptly,
      As on gods, do you gaze on him?'

Who the deepest has thought loves what is most alive,
   Wide experience may well turn to what's best in youth,

      And the wise in the end will
         Often bow to the beautiful.

Friedrich Hölderlin
*Translated from the German
by Michael Hamburger*

To His Mistress

Why dost thou shade thy lovely face? O why
Does that eclipsing hand of thine deny
The sunshine of the Sun's enlivening eye?

Without thy light what light remains in me?
Thou art my life; my way, my light's in thee;
I live, I move, and by thy beams I see.

Thou art my life—if thou but turn away
My life's a thousand deaths. Thou art my way—
Without thee, Love, I travel not but stay.

My light thou art—without thy glorious sight
My eyes are darken'd with eternal night.
My love, thou art my way, my life, my light.

Thou art my way; I wander if thou fly.
Thou art my light; if hid, how blind am I!
Thou art my life; if thou withdraw'st, I die.

My eyes are dark and blind. I cannot see:
To whom or whither should my darkness flee,
But to that light?—and who's that light but thee?

If I have lost my path, dear lover, say,
Shall I still wander in a doubtful way?
Love, shall a lamb of Israel's sheepfold stray?

My path is lost, my wandering steps do stray;
I cannot go, nor can I safely stay;
Whom should I seek but thee, my path, my way?

And yet thou turn'st thy face away and fly'st me!
And yet I sue for grace and thou deny'st me!
Speak, art thou angry, Love, or only try'st me?

Thou art the pilgrim's path, the blind man's eye,
The dead man's life. On thee my hopes rely;
If I but them remove, I surely die.

Dissolve thy sunbeams, close thy wings and stay!
See, see how I am blind, and dead, and stray!
—O thou that art my life, my light, my way!

Then work thy will! If passion bid me flee,
My reason shall obey, my wings shall be
Stretch'd out no farther than from me to thee.

                    John Wilmot, Earl of Rochester

"Go, ill-sped book,
and whisper to her or"

Go, ill-sped book, and whisper to her or
storm out the message for her only ear
that she is beautiful.
Mention sunsets, be not silent of her eyes
and mouth and other prospects, praise her size,
say her figure is full.

Say her small figure is heavenly & full,
so as stunned Henry yatters like a fool
& maketh little sense.
Say she is soft in speech, stately in walking,
modest at gatherings, and in every thing
declare her excellence.

Forget not, when the rest is wholly done
and all her splendours opened one by one
to add that she likes Henry,
for reasons unknown, and fate has bound them fast
one to another in linkages that last
and that are fair to see.

                                        John Berryman

"How do I love thee?
Let me count the ways"

How do I love thee? Let me count the ways.
I love thee to the depth and breadth and height
My soul can reach, when feeling out of sight
For the ends of Being and ideal Grace.
I love thee to the level of everyday's
Most quiet need, by sun and candle light.
I love thee freely, as men strive for Right;
I love thee purely, as they turn from Praise.
I love thee with the passion put to use
In my old griefs, and with my childhood's faith.
I love thee with a love I seemed to lose
With my lost saints—I love thee with the breath,
Smiles, tears, of all my life!—and, if God choose,
I shall but love thee better after death.

                              Elizabeth Barrett Browning

Amoretti I:
"Happy ye leaves! when as those lily hands"

Happy ye leaves! when as those lily hands,
Which hold my life in their dead-doing might,
Shall handle you, and hold in love's soft bands,
Like captives trembling at the victor's sight.
And happy lines! on which, with starry light,
Those lamping eyes will deign sometimes to look,
And read the sorrows of my dying spright,
Written with tears in heart's close-bleeding book.
And happy rhymes! bathed in the sacred brook
Of Helicon, whence she derivèd is,
When ye behold that angel's blessed look.
My soul's long-lackèd food, my heaven's bliss.
Leaves, lines, and rhymes, seek her to please alone,
Whom if ye please, I care for other none.

Edmund Spenser

Luke Havergal

Go to the western gate, Luke Havergal,
There where the vines cling crimson on the wall,
And in the twilight wait for what will come.
The leaves will whisper there of her, and some,
Like flying words, will strike you as they fall;
But go, and if you listen she will call.
Go to the western gate, Luke Havergal—
Luke Havergal.

No, there is not a dawn in eastern skies
To rift the fiery night that's in your eyes;
But there, where western glooms are gathering,
The dark will end the dark, if anything:
God slays Himself with every leaf that flies,
And hell is more than half of paradise.
No, there is not a dawn in eastern skies—
In eastern skies.

Out of a grave I come to tell you this,
Out of a grave I come to quench the kiss
That flames upon your forehead with a glow
That blinds you to the way that you must go.
Yes, there is yet one way to where she is,
Bitter, but one that faith may never miss.
Out of a grave I come to tell you this—
To tell you this.

There is the western gate, Luke Havergal,
There are the crimson leaves upon the wall.
Go, for the winds are tearing them away,—
Nor think to riddle the dead words they say,
Nor any more to feel them as they fall;
But go, and if you trust her she will call.
There is the western gate, Luke Havergal—
Luke Havergal.

                                        E. A. Robinson

The Shepherd's Description of Love

Melibaeus. SHEPHEARD, what's Loue, I pray thee tell?
Faustus.   It is that Fountaine, and that Well,
            Where pleasure and repentance dwell.
            It is perhaps that sauncing bell
                    That tolls all into heauen or hell,
                    And this is Loue as I heard tell.

Meli.   Yet what is Loue, I pre-thee say?
Fau.   It is a worke on holy-day,
        It is December match'd with May,
        When lustie-bloods in fresh array,
                Heare ten moneths after of the play,
                And this is Loue, as I heare say.

Meli.   Yet what is Loue, good Shepheard saine?
Fau.   It is a Sun-shine mixt with raine,
        It is a tooth-ach, or like paine,
        It is a game where none dooth gaine,
                The lasse saith no, and would fall faine:
                And this is Loue, as I heare saine.

Meli.   Yet Shepheard, what is Loue, I pray?
Fau.   It is a yea, It is a nay,
        A pretty kind of sporting fray,
        It is a thing will soone away,
                Then Nimphs take vantage while ye may:
                And this is loue as I heare say.

Meli.   Yet what is Loue, good Shepheard show?
Fau.   A thing that creepes, it cannot goe,
        A prize that passeth too and fro,

A thing for one, a thing for moe,
And he that prooues shall finde it so;
And Shepheard this is loue I troe.

Sir Walter Raleigh

The Guest

Everything as before: blown snow
beats against the dining-room windows.
I have not changed,
but a man came to me.

I asked, 'What do you want?'
He said, 'To be with you in hell.'
I laughed, 'No doubt you'll
ruin us both.'

But he lifted his thin hand
and softly touched the flowers:
'Tell me how they kiss you,
tell me how you kiss.'

His dull eyes looked
fixedly at my ring.
Not a single muscle moved
in his radiant, evil face.

Oh, I know: it is his delight
to know intensely and passionately,
that he needs nothing,
that I can refuse him nothing.

Anna Akhmatova
*Translated from the Russian
by Richard McKane*

143

My dearest Girl,

This moment I have set myself to copy some verses out fair. I cannot proceed with any degree of content. I must write you a line or two and see if that will assist in dismissing you from my Mind for ever so short a time. Upon my Soul I can think of nothing else—The time is passed when I had power to advise and warn you again[s]t the unpromising morning of my Life—My love has made me selfish. I cannot exist without you—I am forgetful of every thing but seeing you again—my Life seems to stop there —I see no further. You have absorb'd me. I have a sensation at the present moment as though I was dissolving—I should be exquisitely miserable without the hope of soon seeing you. I should be affraid to separate myself far from you. My sweet Fanny, will your heart never change? My love, will it? I have no limit now to my love—You note came in just here—I cannot be happier away from you—'T is richer than an Argosy of Pearles. Do not threat me even in jest. I have been astonished that Men could die Martyrs for religion—I have shudder'd at it—I shudder no more —I could be martyr'd for my Religion—Love is my religion—I could die for that—I could die for you. My Creed is Love and you are its only tenet—You have ravish'd me away by a Power I cannot resist: and yet I could resist till I saw you; and even since I have seen you I have endeavoured often "to reason against the reasons of my Love." I can do that no more—the pain would be too great—My Love is selfish—I cannot breathe without you.

Yours for ever

John Keats

Letter from John Keats
to Fanny Brawne, 13 October 1819.

Epithalamion

Ye learnèd sisters, which have oftentimes
Beene to me ayding, others to adorne,
Whom ye thought worthy of your gracefull rymes,
That even the greatest did not greatly scorne
To heare theyr names sung in your simple layes,
But joyèd in theyr praise;
And when ye list your owne mishaps to mourne,
Which death, or love, or fortunes wreck did rayse,
Your string could soone to sadder tenor turne,
And teach the woods and waters to lament
Your dolefull dreriment:
Now lay those sorrowfull complaints aside;
And, having all your heads with girlands crownd,
Helpe me mine owne loves prayses to resound;
Ne let the same of any be envide:
So Orpheus did for his owne bride!
So I unto my selfe alone will sing;
The woods shall to me answer, and my Eccho ring.

Early, before the worlds light-giving lampe
His golden beame upon the hils doth spred,
Having disperst the nights unchearefull dampe,
Doe ye awake; and, with fresh lusty-hed,
Go to the bowre of my belovèd love,
My truest turtle dove;
Bid her awake; for Hymen is awake,
And long since ready forth his maske to move,
With his bright Tead that flames with many a flake,
And many a bachelor to waite on him,
In theyr fresh garments trim.
Bid her awake therefore, and soone her dight,

145

For lo! the wishèd day is come at last,
That shall, for all the paynes and sorrowes past,
Pay to her usury of long delight:
And, whylest she doth her dight,
Doe ye to her of joy and solace sing,
That all the woods may answer, and your eccho ring.

Bring with you all the Nymphes that you can heare
Both of the rivers and the forrests greene,
And of the sea that neighbours to her neare:
Al with gay girlands goodly wel beseene.
And let them also with them bring in hand
Another gay girland
For my fayre love, of lillyes and of roses,
Bound truelove wize, with a blew silke riband.
And let them make great store of bridale poses,
And let them eeke bring store of other flowers,
To deck the bridale bowers.
And let the ground whereas her foot shall tread,
For feare the stones her tender foot should wrong,
Be strewed with fragrant flowers all along,
And diapred lyke the discolored mead.
Which done, doe at her chamber dore awayt,
For she will waken strayt;
The whiles doe ye this song unto her sing,
The woods shall to you answer, and your Eccho ring.

Ye Nymphes of Mulla, which with carefull heed
The silver scaly trouts doe tend full well,
And greedy pikes which use therein to feed;
(Those trouts and pikes all others doo excell;)
And ye likewise, which keepe the rushy lake,
Where none doo fishes take;
Bynd up the locks the which hang scatterd light,
And in his waters, which your mirror make,
Behold your faces as the christall bright,
That when you come whereas my love doth lie,

No blemish she may spie.
And eke, ye lightfoot mayds, which keepe the deere,
That on the hoary mountayne used to towre;
And the wylde wolves, which seeke them to devoure,
With your steele darts doo chace from comming neer;
Be also present heere,
To helpe to decke her, and to help to sing,
That all the woods may answer, and your eccho ring.

Wake now, my love, awake! for it is time;
The Rosy Morne long since left Tithones bed,
All ready to her silver coche to clyme;
And Phœbus gins to shew his glorious hed.
Hark! how the cheerefull birds do chaunt theyr laies
And carroll of Loves praise.
The merry Larke hir mattins sings aloft;
The Thrush replyes; the Mavis descant playes;
The Ouzell shrills; the Ruddock warbles soft;
So goodly all agree, with sweet consent,
To this dayes merriment.
Ah! my deere love, why doe ye sleepe thus long?
When meeter were that ye should now awake,
T' awayt the comming of your joyous make,
And hearken to the birds love-learnèd song,
The deawy leaves among!
Nor they of joy and pleasance to you sing,
That all the woods them answer, and theyr eccho ring.

My love is now awake out of her dreames,
And her fayre eyes, like stars that dimmèd were
With darksome cloud, now shew theyr goodly beams
More bright then Hesperus his head doth rere.
Come now, ye damzels, daughters of delight,
Helpe quickly her to dight:
But first come ye fayre houres, which were begot
In Joves sweet paradice of Day and Night;
Which doe the seasons of the yeare allot,

147

And al, that ever in this world is fayre,
Doe make and still repayre:
And ye three handmayds of the Cyprian Queene,
The which doe still adorne her beauties pride,
Helpe to addorne my beautifullest bride:
And, as ye her array, still throw betweene
Some graces to be seene;
And, as ye use to Venus, to her sing,
The whiles the woods shal answer, and your eccho ring.

Now is my love all ready forth to come:
Let all the virgins therefore well awayt:
And ye fresh boyes, that tend upon her groome,
Prepare your selves; for he is comming strayt.
Set all your things in seemely good aray,
Fit for so joyfull day:
The joyfulst day that ever sunne did see.
Faire Sun! shew forth thy favourable ray,
And let thy lifull heat not fervent be,
For feare of burning her sunshyny face,
Her beauty to disgrace.
O fayrest Phœbus! father of the Muse!
If ever I did honour thee aright,
Or sing the thing that mote thy mind delight,
Doe not thy servants simple boone refuse;
But let this day, let this one day, be myne;
Let all the rest be thine.
Then *I* thy soverayne prayses loud wil sing,
That all the woods shal answer, and theyr eccho ring.

Harke! how the Minstrils gin to shrill aloud
Their merry Musick that resounds from far,
The pipe, the tabor, and the trembling Croud,
That well agree withouten breach or jar.
But, most of all, the Damzels doe delite
When they their tymbrels smyte,
And thereunto doe daunce and carrol sweet,
That all the sences they doe ravish quite;
The whyles the boyes run up and downe the street,
Crying aloud with strong confusèd noyce,
As if it were one voyce,
Hymen, iö Hymen, Hymen, they do shout;
That even to the heavens theyr shouting shrill
Doth reach, and all the firmament doth fill;
To which the people standing all about,
As in approvance, doe thereto applaud,
And loud advaunce her laud;

149

And evermore they Hymen, Hymen sing,
That al the woods them answer, and theyr eccho ring.

Loe! where she comes along with portly pace,
Lyke Phœbe, from her chamber of the East,
Arysing forth to run her mighty race,
Clad all in white, that seemes a virgin best.
So well it her beseemes, that ye would weene
Some angell she had beene.
Her long loose yellow locks lyke golden wyre,
Sprinckled with perle, and perling flowres atweene,
Doe lyke a golden mantle her attyre;
And, being crownèd with a girland greene,
Seeme lyke some mayden Queene.
Her modest eyes, abashèd to behold
So many gazers as on her do stare,
Upon the lowly ground affixèd are;
Ne dare lift up her countenance too bold,
But blush to heare her prayses sung so loud,
So farre from being proud.
Nathlesse doe ye still loud her prayses sing,
That all the woods may answer, and your eccho ring.

Tell me, ye merchants daughters, did ye see
So fayre a creature in your towne before;
So sweet, so lovely, and so mild as she,
Adornd with beautyes grace and vertues store?
Her goodly eyes lyke Saphyres shining bright,
Her forehead yvory white,
Her cheekes lyke apples which the sun hath rudded,
Her lips lyke cherryes charming men to byte,
Her brest like to a bowle of creame uncrudded,
Her paps lyke lyllies budded,
Her snowie necke lyke to a marble towre;
And all her body like a pallace fayre,
Ascending up, with many a stately stayre,
To honors seat and chastities sweet bowre.

Why stand ye still ye virgins in amaze,
Upon her so to gaze,
Whiles ye forget your former lay to sing,
To which the woods did answer, and your eccho ring?

But if ye saw that which no eyes can see,
The inward beauty of her lively spright,
Garnisht with heavenly guifts of high degree,
Much more then would ye wonder at that sight,
And stand astonisht lyke to those which red
Medusaes mazeful hed.
There dwels sweet love, and constant chastity,
Unspotted fayth, and comely womanhood,
Regard of honour, and mild modesty;
There vertue raynes as Queene in royal throne,
And giveth lawes alone,
The which the base affections doe obay,
And yeeld theyr services unto her will;
Ne thought of thing uncomely ever may
Thereto approch to tempt her mind to ill.
Had ye once seene these her celestial threasures,
And unrevealèd pleasures,
Then would ye wonder, and her prayses sing,
That al the woods should answer, and your echo ring.

Open the temple gates unto my love,
Open them wide that she may enter in,
And all the postes adorne as doth behove,
And all the pillours deck with girlands trim,
For to receyve this Saynt with honour dew,
That commeth in to you.
With trembling steps, and humble reverence,
She commeth in, before th' Almighties view;
Of her ye virgins learne obedience,
When so ye come into those holy places,
To humble your proud faces:
Bring her up to th' high altar, that she may

The sacred ceremonies there partake,
The which do endlesse matrimony make;
And let the roring Organs loudly play
The praises of the Lord in lively notes;
The whiles, with hollow throates,
The Choristers the joyous Antheme sing,
That al the woods may answere, and their eccho ring.

Behold, whiles she before the altar stands,
Hearing the holy priest that to her speakes,
And blesseth her with his two happy hands,
How the red roses flush up in her cheekes,
And the pure snow, with goodly vermill stayne
Like crimsin dyde in grayne:
That even th' Angels, which continually
About the sacred Altare doe remaine,
Forget their service and about her fly,
Ofte peeping in her face, that seems more fayre,
The more they on it stare.
But her sad eyes, still fastened on the ground,
Are governèd with goodly modesty,
That suffers not one looke to glaunce awry,
Which may let in a little thought unsownd.
Why blush ye, love, to give to me your hand,
The pledge of all our band!
Sing, ye sweet Angels, Alleluya sing,
That all the woods may answere, and your eccho ring.

Now al is done: bring home the bride againe;
Bring home the triumph of our victory:
Bring home with you the glory of her gaine;
With joyance bring her and with jollity.
Never had man more joyfull day then this,
Whom heaven would heape with blis,
Make feast therefore now all this live-long day;
This day for ever to me holy is.
Poure out the wine without restraint or stay,
Poure not by cups, but by the belly full,
Poure out to all that wull,
And sprinkle all the postes and wals with wine,
That they may sweat, and drunken be withall.
Crowne ye God Bacchus with a coronall,
And Hymen also crowne with wreathes of vine;
And let the Graces daunce unto the rest,
For they can doo it best:

The whiles the maydens doe theyr carroll sing,
To which the woods shall answer, and theyr eccho ring.

Ring ye the bels, ye yong men of the towne,
And leave your wonted labors for this day:
This day is holy; doe ye write it downe,
That ye for ever it remember may.
This day the sunne is in his chiefest hight,
With Barnaby the bright,
From whence declining daily by degrees,
He somewhat loseth of his heat and light,
When once the Crab behind his back he sees.
But for this time it ill ordainèd was,
To chose the longest day in all the yeare,
And shortest night, when longest fitter weare:
Yet never day so long, but late would passe.
Ring ye the bels, to make it weare away,
And bonefiers make all day;
And daunce about them, and about them sing,
That all the woods may answer, and your eccho ring.

Ah! when will this long weary day have end,
And lende me leave to come unto my love?
How slowly do the houres theyr numbers spend?
How slowly does sad Time his feathers move?
Hast thee, O fayrest Planet, to thy home,
Within the Westerne fome:
Thy tyrèd steedes long since have need of rest.
Long though it be, at last I see it gloome,
And the bright evening-star with golden creast
Appeare out of the East.
Fayre childe of beauty! glorious lampe of love!
That all the host of heaven in rankes doost lead,
And guydest lovers through the nights sad dread,
How chearefully thou lookest from above,
And seemst to laugh atweene thy twinkling light,
As joying in the sight

Of these glad many, which for joy doe sing,
That all the woods them answer, and their echo ring!

Now ceasse, ye damsels, your delights fore-past;
Enough it is that all the day was youres:
Now day is doen, and night is nighing fast,
Now bring the Bryde into the brydall boures.
The night is come, now soon her disaray,
And in her bed her lay;
Lay her in lillies and in violets,
And silken courteins over her display,
And odourd sheetes, and Arras coverlets.
Behold how goodly my faire love does ly,
In proud humility!
Like unto Maia, when as Jove her took
In Tempe, lying on the flowry gras,
Twixt sleepe and wake, after she weary was,
With bathing in the Acidalian brooke.
Now it is night, ye damsels may be gon,
And leave my love alone,
And leave likewise your former lay to sing:
The woods no more shall answere, nor your echo ring.

Now welcome, night! thou night so long expected,
That long daies labour doest at last defray,
And all my cares, which cruell Love collected,
Hast sumd in one, and cancellèd for aye:
Spread thy broad wing over my love and me,
That no man may us see;
And in thy sable mantle us enwrap,
From feare of perrill and foule horror free.
Let no false treason seeke us to entrap,
Nor any dread disquiet once annoy
The safety of our joy;
But let the night be calme, and quietsome,
Without tempestuous storms or sad afray:
Lyke as when Jove with fayre Alcmena lay,

When he begot the great Tirynthian groome:
Or lyke as when he with thy selfe did lie
And begot Majesty.
And let the mayds and yong men cease to sing;
Ne let the woods them answer nor theyr eccho ring.

Let no lamenting cryes, nor dolefull teares,
Be heard all night within, nor yet without:
Ne let false whispers, breeding hidden feares,
Breake gentle sleepe with misconceivèd dout.
Let no deluding dreames, nor dreadfull sights,
Make sudden sad affrights;
Ne let house-fyres, nor lightnings helplesse harmes,
Ne let the Pouke, nor other evill sprights,
Ne let mischivous witches with theyr charmes,
Ne let hob Goblins, names whose sence we see not,
Fray us with things that be not:
Let not the shriech Oule nor the Storke be heard,
Nor the night Raven, that still deadly yels;
Nor damnèd ghosts, cald up with mighty spels,
Nor griesly vultures, make us once affeard:
Ne let th' unpleasant Quyre of Frogs still croking
Make us to wish theyr choking.
Let none of these theyr drery accents sing;
Ne let the woods them answer, nor theyr eccho ring.

But let stil Silence trew night-watches keepe,
That sacred Peace may in assurance rayne,
And tymely Sleep, when it is tyme to sleepe,
May poure his limbs forth on your pleasant playne;
The whiles an hundred little wingèd loves,
Like divers-fethered doves,
Shall fly and flutter round about your bed,
And in the secret darke, that none reproves,
Their prety stealthes shal worke, and snares shal spread
To filch away sweet snatches of delight,
Conceald through covert night.

156

Ye sonnes of Venus, play your sports at will!
For greedy pleasure, carelesse of your toyes,
Thinks more upon her paradise of joyes,
Then what ye do, albe it good or ill.
All night therefore attend your merry play,
For it will soone be day:
Now none doth hinder you, that say or sing;
Ne will the woods now answer, nor your Eccho ring.

Who is the same, which at my window peepes?
Or whose is that faire face that shines so bright?
Is it not Cinthia, she that never sleepes,
But walkes about high heaven al the night?
O! fayrest goddesse, do thou not envy
My love with me to spy:
For thou likewise didst love, though now unthought,
And for a fleece of wooll, which privily
The Latmian shepherd once unto thee brought,
His pleasures with thee wrought.
Therefore to us be favorable now;
And sith of wemens labours thou hast charge,
And generation goodly dost enlarge,
Encline thy will t'effect our wishfull vow,
And the chast wombe informe with timely seed
That may our comfort breed:
Till which we cease our hopefull hap to sing;
Ne let the woods us answere, nor our Eccho ring.

And thou, great Juno! which with awful might
The lawes of wedlock still dost patronize;
And the religion of the faith first plight
With sacred rites hast taught to solemnize;
And eeke for comfort often callèd art
Of women in their smart;
Eternally bind thou this lovely band,
And all thy blessings unto us impart.
And thou, glad Genius! in whose gentle hand

The bridale bowre and geniall bed remaine,
Without blemish or staine;
And the sweet pleasures of theyr loves delight
With secret ayde doest succour and supply,
Till they bring forth the fruitfull progeny;
Send us the timely fruit of this same night.
And thou, fayre Hebe! and thou, Hymen free!
Grant that it may so be.
Til which we cease your further prayse to sing;
Ne any woods shall answer, nor your Eccho ring.

And ye high heavens, the temple of the gods,
In which a thousand torches flaming bright
Doe burne, that to us wretched earthly clods
In dreadful darknesse lend desirèd light
And all ye powers which in the same remayne,
More then we men can fayne!
Poure out your blessing on us plentiously,
And happy influence upon us raine,
That we may raise a large posterity,
Which from the earth, which they may long possesse
With lasting happinesse,
Up to your haughty pallaces may mount;
And, for the guerdon of theyr glorious merit,
May heavenly tabernacles there inherit,
Of blessèd Saints for to increase the count.
So let us rest, sweet love, in hope of this,
And cease till then our tymely joyes to sing:
The woods no more us answer, nor our eccho ring!

Song! made in lieu of many ornaments,
With which my love should duly have been dect,
Which cutting off through hasty accidents,
Ye would not stay your dew time to expect,
But promist both to recompens;
Be unto her a goodly ornament,
And for short time an endlesse moniment.

Edmund Spenser

6

"O the sweet cry, the dark eye!
Love stamps its foot but cannot slip the knot."

St. Valentine

A woman's breasts
for beauty
A man's delights
for charm

The rod and cups
of duty
to stave us
from harm!

A woman's eyes
a woman's
thighs and a man's
straight look:

Cities rotted to
pig-sties
will stand up by
that book!

William Carlos Williams

161

The Accomplices

A love I love whose lips I love
but conscience she has none
nor can I rest upon her breast
for faith's to her unknown
light-hearted to my bed she comes
but she is early gone.

This lady in the sunlight is
as magic as the sun
and in my arms and all night long
she seems and is my own
yet but a Monday love is she
and Tuesday she is gone.

Rare as charity is her hand
that rests my heart upon
but charity to so many kind
stays for a day with none
a spendthrift love she spends her love
and all will soon be gone.

Yet though my trust has been betrayed
reproaches have I none
no heart but is of treason made
or has not mischief done
and we could be together false
if she would but stay on.

Conrad Aiken

"The Way I read a Letter's—this"

The Way I read a Letter's—this—
'Tis first—I lock the Door—
And push it with my fingers—next—
For transport it be sure—

And then I go the furthest off
To counteract a knock—
Then draw my little Letter forth
And slowly pick the lock—

Then—glancing narrow at the Wall—
And narrow at the floor
For firm Conviction of a Mouse
Not exorcised before—

Peruse how infinite I am
To no one that You—know—
And sigh for lack of Heaven—but not
The Heaven God bestow—

Emily Dickinson

"I serve a mistress whiter than the snow"

I serve a mistress whiter than the snow,
   Straighter than cedar, brighter than the glass,
Finer in trip and swifter than the roe,
   More pleasant than the field of flowering grass;
More gladsome to my withering joys that fade
Than winter's sun or summer's cooling shade.

Sweeter than swelling grape of ripest wine,
  Softer than feathers of the fairest swan,
Smoother than jet, more stately than the pine,
  Fresher than poplar, smaller than my span,
Clearer than beauty's fiery-pointed beam,
Or icy crust of crystal's frozen stream.

Yet is she curster than the bear by kind,
  And harder-hearted than the agèd oak,
More glib than oil, more fickle than the wind,
  Stiffer than steel, no sooner bent but broke.
Lo, thus my service is a lasting sore;
Yet will I serve, although I die therefore.

Anthony Munday

"Madame, withouten many words"

Madame, withouten many words,
Once, I am sure, ye will or no.
And if ye will, then leave your bords,
And use your wit, and show it so;
And with a beck ye shall me call;
And if of one that burneth alway
Ye have any pity at all,
Answer him fair with yea or nay.
If it be yea, I shall be fain;
If it be nay, friends as before.
Ye shall another man obtain
And I mine own, and yours no more.

Sir Thomas Wyatt

"Venus, with young Adonis sitting by her"

Venus, with young Adonis sitting by her
Under a myrtle shade, began to woo him:
She told the youngling how god Mars did try her.
And as he fell to her, so fell she to him.
"Even thus," quoth she, "the warlike god embraced me,"
And then she clipped Adonis in her arms;
"Even thus," quoth she, "the warlike god unlaced me,"
As if the boy should use like loving charms;
"Even thus," quoth she, "he seizéd on my lips,"
And with her lips on his did act the seizure:
And as she fetchéd breath, away he skips,
And would not take her meaning nor her pleasure.
Ah, that I had my lady at this bay,
To kiss and clip me till I run away!

Bartholomew Griffin

Sonnet XCIV: "They that have power to hurt and will do none"

They that have power to hurt and will do none,
That do not do the thing they most do show;
Who, moving others, are themselves as stone,
Unmoved, cold and to temptation slow;
They rightly do inherit heaven's graces
And husband nature's riches from expense;
They are the lords and owners of their faces.
Others but stewards of their excellence.
The summer's flower is to the summer sweet,
Though to itself it only live and die,

But if that flower with base infection meet,
The basest weed outbraves his dignity:
For sweetest things turn sourest by their deeds;
Lilies that fester smell far worse than weeds.

William Shakespeare

Love and a Question

A Stranger came to the door at eve,
    And he spoke the bridegroom fair.
He bore a green-white stick in his hand,
    And, for all burden, care.
He asked with the eyes more than the lips
    For a shelter for the night,
And he turned and looked at the road afar
    Without a window light.

The bridegroom came forth into the porch
    With 'Let us look at the sky,
And question what of the night to be,
    Stranger, you and I.'
The woodbine leaves littered the yard,
    The woodbine berries were blue,
Autumn, yes, winter was in the wind;
    'Stranger, I wish I knew.'

Within, the bride in the dusk alone
    Bent over the open fire,
Her face rose-red with the glowing coal
    And the thought of the heart's desire.
The bridegroom looked at the weary road,
    Yet saw but her within,
And wished her heart in a case of gold
    And pinned with a silver pin.

The bridegroom thought it little to give
   A dole of bread, a purse,
A heartfelt prayer for the poor of God,
   Or for the rich a curse;
But whether or not a man was asked
   To mar the love of two
By harboring woe in the bridal house,
   The bridegroom wished he knew.

Robert Frost

Dream

I called you. You called me.
We gushed forth like rivers,
and there arose to heaven
our two names commingled.

I called you. You called me.
We gushed forth like rivers.
Our bodies still remained
face to face quite empty.

I called you. You called me.
We gushed forth like rivers,
but between our bodies
what unforgettable chasm!

Emilio Prados
*Translated from the Spanish
by Eleanor L. Turnbull*

167

I'm Owre Young to Marry Yet

I am my mammie's ae bairn,
   Wi' unco folk I weary, Sir;
And lying in a man's bed,
   I'm fley'd wad mak me eerie, Sir.

I'm owre young, I'm owre young,
   I'm owre young to marry yet;
I'm owre young, 'twad be a sin
   To tak me frae my mammie yet.

My mammie coft me a new gown,
   The kirk maun hae the gracing o't;
Were I to lie wi' you, kind Sir,
   I'm fear'd ye'd spoil the lacing o't. . . .

Hallowmas is come and gane,
   The nights are lang in winter, Sir;
And you an' I in ae bed,
   In truth I dare na venture, Sir. . . .

Fu' loud and shrill the frosty wind
   Blaws thro' the leafless timmer, Sir;
But if ye come this gate again,
   I'll aulder be gin simmer, Sir.

I'm owre young, I'm owre young,
   I'm owre young to marry yet;
I'm owre young, 'twad be a sin
   To tak me frae my mammie yet.

Robert Burns

168

Fidessa XXIII: "Fly to her heart; hover about her heart"

Fly to her heart; hover about her heart.
With dainty kisses mollify her heart.
Pierce with thy arrows her obdurate heart.
With sweet allurements ever move her heart.
At midday and at midnight touch her heart.
Be lurking closely, nestle about her heart.
With power (thou art a god!) command her heart.
Kindle thy coals of love about her heart.
Yea, even into thyself transform her heart,
Ah, she must love! Be sure thou have her heart.
And I must die, if thou have not her heart.
Thy bed, if thou rest well, must be her heart.
He hath the best part, sure, that hath her heart;
What have I not, if I have but her heart!

Bartholomew Griffin

The Lawn

Wo'd I see Lawn, clear as the Heaven, and thin?
It sh'd be onely in my Julia's skin:
Which so betrayes her blood, as we discover
The blush of cherries, when a Lawn's cast over.

Robert Herrick

Song from *Marriage-a-la-Mode*

Whil'st *Alexis* lay prest
In her Arms, he lov'd best,
With his hands round her neck,
And his head on her breast,
He found the fierce pleasure too hasty to stay,
And his soul in the tempest just flying away.

When *Coelia* saw this,
With a sigh, and a kiss,
She cry'd, Oh my dear, I am robb'd of my bliss;
'Tis unkind to your Love, and unfaithfully done,
To leave me behind you, and die all alone.

The Youth though in haste,
And breathing his last,
In pity dy'd slowly, while she dy'd more fast;
Till at length she cry'd, Now, my dear, now let us go,
Now die, my *Alexis*, and I will die too.

Thus intranc'd they did lie,
Till *Alexis* did try
To recover new breath, that again he might die:
Then often they di'd; but the more they did so,
The Nymph di'd more quick, and the Shepherd more slow.

John Dryden

Six Kisses

(after Rodin's "The Kiss")

1

No longer itself
the hand on that bare thigh
becomes the woman it touches.
The two merge in the hush.
Their skin sweats through the stone.

2

She brings news to the blood,
promises to the mouth.
Their ruly hairs combine.
For once, nothing is wrong.

3

The parts in touching kiss
and in parting touch on what it is
a kiss is.

4

Who speaks? No one.
The tongue, ripe as a noun,
tastes of poems.

The arch of arm, the foot's arch.
Every nerve confides in another.
The mouth was made for such involvement.
This kiss causes them wonder, causes them
panic, joy.

6

They are each other.

Nancy Sullivan

Late Air

From a magician's midnight sleeve
        the radio-singers
distribute all their love-songs
over the dew-wet lawns.
        And like a fortune-teller's
their marrow-piercing guesses are whatever you believe.

But on the Navy Yard aerial I find
        better witnesses
for love on summer nights.
Five remote red lights
        keep their nests there; Phoenixes
burning quietly, where the dew cannot climb.

Elizabeth Bishop

The Dreame

Deare love, for nothing lesse then thee
Would I have broke this happy dreame,
　　　It was a theame
For reason, much too strong for phantasie,
Therefore, thou wakd'st me wisely; yet
My Dreame thou brok'st not, but continued'st it,
Thou art so truth, that thoughts of thee suffice,
To make dreames truths; and fables histories;
Enter these armes, for since thou thoughtst it best,
Not to dreame all my dreame, let's act the rest.

As lightning, or a Tapers light,
Thine eyes, and not thy noise wak'd mee;
　　　Yet I thought thee
(For thou lovest truth) an Angell, at first sight,
But when I saw thou sawest my heart,
And knew'st my thoughts, beyond an Angels art,
When thou knew'st what I dreamt, when thou knew'st
Excesse of joy would wake me, and cam'st then, when
I must confesse, it could not chuse but bee
Prophane, to thinke thee any thing but thee.

Comming and staying show'd thee, thee,
But rising makes me doubt, that now,
　　　Thou art not thou.
That love is weake, where feare's as strong as hee;
'Tis not all spirit, pure, and brave,
If mixture it of FEARE, SHAME, HONOR, have.
Perchance as torches which must ready bee,
Men light and put out, so thou deal'st with mee,
Thou cam'st to kindle, goest to come; Then I
Will dreame that hope againe, but else would die.

John Donne

Adolescent's Song

Lopsided love in hotel rooms,
And desperate love, asleep in tombs,
And hour-glass brides and mock bridegrooms,
Are not the pure friends that once were we,
O Timothy, Timothy, Timothy.

The mirror man and the paramour,
And broken glass on the slanting floor,
And the midnight punk and the drunken whore,
Are not the pure friends that once were we,
O Timothy, Timothy, Timothy.

The vacant loves in apartment halls,
And boys for boys and girls for girls,
And the wilted love that pays the bills,
Are not the pure friends that once were we,
O Timothy, Timothy, Timothy.

Goodbye. Bon soir. Farewell. So long.
The singer is parted from his song.
To whom should the singer's song be sung?
Not the pure friend that once you were,
Timothy.

Howard Moss

The Good-Morrow

I Wonder by my troth, what thou, and I
Did, till we lov'd? were we not wean'd till then?
But suck'd on countrey pleasures, childishly?
Or snorted we in the seaven sleepers den?
T'was so; But this, all pleasures fancies bee.
If ever any beauty I did see,
Which I desir'd, and got, t'was but a dreame of thee.

And now good morrow to our waking soules,
Which watch not one another out of feare;
For love, all love of other sights controules,
And makes one little roome, an every where.
Let sea discoverers to new worlds have gone,
Let Maps to other, worlds on worlds have showne,
Let us possesse one world, each hath one, and is one.

My face in thine eye, thine in mine appeares,
And true plaine hearts doe in the faces rest,
Where can we finde two better hemispheares
Without sharpe North, without declining West?
What ever dyes, was not mixt equally;
If our two loves be one, or, thou and I
Love so alike, that none doe slacken, none can die.

John Donne

"The lark now leaves his watery nest"

The lark now leaves his watery nest,
  And climbing shakes his dewy wings;
He takes this window for the East,
  And to implore your light he sings—
Awake, awake, the morn will never rise
Till she can dress her beauty at your eyes.

The merchant bows unto the seaman's star,
  The ploughman from the sun his season takes;
But still the lover wonders what they are
  Who look for day before his mistress wakes.
Awake, awake! break through your veils of lawn!
Then draw your curtains, and begin the dawn!

Sir William Davenant

Her Leg

Fain would I kiss my Julia's dainty Leg,
Which is as white and hair-less as an egge.

Robert Herrick

To Mistress Margaret Hussey

Merry Margaret,
    As midsummer flower,
Gentle as falcon
Or hawk of the tower:
With solace and gladness,
Much mirth and no madness,
All good and no badness;
    So joyously,
    So maidenly,
    So womanly
    Her demeaning
    In every thing,
    Far, far passing
    That I can indite,
    Or suffice to write
Of Merry Margaret
    As midsummer flower,
Gentle as falcon
Or hawk of the tower.
    As patient and still
And as full of good will
As fair Isaphill,
Coriander,
Sweet pomander,
Good Cassander,
Steadfast of thought,
Well made, well wrought,
Far may be sought
Ere that ye can find
So courteous, so kind

As Merry Margaret,
    This midsummer flower,
Gentle as falcon
Or hawk of the tower.

John Skelton

"Thy fingers make early flowers of"

Thy fingers make early flowers of
all things.
thy hair mostly the hours love:
a smoothness which
sings, saying
(though love be a day)
do not fear, we will go amaying.

thy whitest feet crisply are straying.
Always
thy moist eyes are at kisses playing,
whose strangeness much
says; singing
(though love be a day)
for which girl art thou flowers bringing?

To be thy lips is a sweet thing
and small.
Death, thee i call rich beyond wishing
if this thou catch,
else missing.
(though love be a day
and life be nothing, it shall not stop kissing).

E. E. Cummings

179

Sonnet VII: "And so one sees
all living matter perish"

And so one sees all living matter perish
    As soon as its elusive breath has gone.
    You are the breath; I am the blood and bone.
    O heart, which I so desperately cherish,
Where have you vanished? Do not leave me lost,
    Pale and imperiled! O, come back again,
    Bring back this broken body from its pain,
    Return its precious and essential ghost!
But then, contrive it somehow without danger,
    O love, this wild and terrifying meeting,
    This hot return; and let me give my greeting
In calm and coolness to this mighty stranger;
    And let his warming loveliness enfold
    Me gently, who was once so bitter cold.

Louise Labé
*Translated from the French
by Frederic Prokosch*

"There is a white mare that my love keeps"

There is a white mare that my love keeps
unridden in a hillside meadow—white
as a white pebble, veined like a stone
a white horse, whiter than a girl.

And now for three nights sleeping I have seen
her body naked as a tree for marriage
pale as a stone that the net of water covers

and her veined breasts like hills—the swallow islands
still on the corn's green water: and I know
her dark hairs gathered round an open rose

her pebbles lying under the dappled sea.
And I will ride her thighs' white horses.

Alex Comfort

Reward of Service

"A knight there is," a lady said,
"Hath served me as I wished full fain.
Or ere the time of year be fled,
His due reward he needs must gain.
Now snow and winter seem to me
Flower and clover fair to be,
When in my arms I hold him fast.
Though all the world should take it ill,
Yet must he get his will at last!"

Anonymous
*Translated from medieval German
by F. C. Nicholson*

On a Statue of Venus

From Venus' breast a bit of greenery grows.
Where fire is pulsing deep, the marble knows.

Anonymous

The Falcon

I raised a noble falcon
For more than a year;
And when I had tamed him
And decked his feathers, tying
Them with a golden band,
He rose so swiftly, flying
Far to another land.
Since then I've seen my falcon
Gaily soaring;
And from his feet were waving
Fair silken ribbons,
And on his wings each feather
Was ruddy gold to see;
Ah, God bring those together
Who lovers fain would be!

The Knight of Kürenberg
*Translated from medieval German
by Margarete Münsterberg*

Poems of Night

1

I touch your face,
I move my hand over
Slopes, falls, lumps of sight,
Lashes barely able to be touched,
Lips that give way so easily
It's a shock to feel underneath
The hard grin of the bones.

Muffled a little, barely cloaked,
Zygoma, maxillary, turbinate.

2

I put my hand
On the side of your face,
You lean your head a little
Into my hand—and so,
I know you're a dormouse
Taken up in winter sleep,
A lonely, stunned weight
Shut in the natural mystery.

3

A cheekbone,
A curved piece of brow,
A pale eyelid
Float in the dark,
And now I make out
An eye, dark,
Wormed with far-off, unaccountable lights.

4

Hardly touching, I hold
What I can only think of
As some deepest of memories in my arms,
Not mine, but as if the life in me
Were slowly remembering what it is.

You lie here now in your physicalness,
This beautiful degree of reality.

5

And now the day, raft that breaks up, comes on.

I think of a few bones
Floating on a river at night,
The starlight blowing in place on the water,
The river leaning like a wave towards the emptiness.

Galway Kinnell

Meeting at Night

I

The grey sea and the long black land;
And the yellow half-moon large and low;
And the startled little waves that leap
In fiery ringlets from their sleep,
As I gain the cove with pushing prow,
And quench its speed i' the slushy sand.

II

Then a mile of warm sea-scented beach;
Three fields to cross till a farm appears;
A tap at the pane, the quick sharp scratch
And blue spurt of a lighted match,
And a voice less loud, thro' its joys and fears,
Than the two hearts beating each to each!

Parting at Morning

Round the cape of a sudden came the sea,
And the sun looked over the mountain's rim:
And straight was a path of gold for him,
And the need of a world of men for me.

Robert Browning

Astrophel and Stella 39: "Come sleep! O sleep, the certain knot of peace"

Come sleep! O sleep, the certain knot of peace,
　　The baiting place of wit, the balm of woe,
　　The poor man's wealth, the prisoner's release,
　　Th' indifferent judge between the high and low;
With shield of proof shield me from out the prease
　　Of those fierce darts despair at me doth throw;
　　O make in me those civil wars to cease;
　　I will good tribute pay, if thou do so.
Take thou of me smooth pillows, sweetest bed,
　　A chamber deaf to noise and blind to light,
　　A rosy garland and a weary head;
And if these things, as being thine by right,
　　Move not thy heavy grace, thou shalt in me,
　　Livelier than elsewhere, Stella's image see.

Sir Philip Sidney

Spirit's Song

How well you served me above ground,
Most truthful sight, firm-builded sound.

And how you throve through hunger, waste,
Sickness and health, informing taste;

And smell, that did from dung and heather,
Corruption, bloom, mix well together.

185

But you, fierce delicate tender touch,
Betrayed and hurt me overmuch,

For whom I lagged with what a crew
O far too long, and poisoned through!

Louise Bogan

"Mine—by the Right of the White Election!"

Mine—by the Right of the White Election!
Mine—by the Royal Seal!
Mine—by the Sign in the Scarlet prison—
Bars—cannot conceal!

Mine—here—in Vision—and in Veto!
Mine—by the Grave's Repeal—
Titled—Confirmed—
Delirious Charter!
Mine—long as Ages steal!

Emily Dickinson

"Surprised by joy—impatient as the Wind"

Surprised by joy—impatient as the Wind
I turned to share the transport—Oh! with whom
But Thee, deep buried in the silent tomb,
That spot which no vicissitude can find?
Love, faithful love, recalled thee to my mind—
But how could I forget thee? Through what power,
Even for the least division of an hour,

186

Have I been so beguiled as to be blind
To my most grievous loss!—That thought's return
Was the worst pang that sorrow ever bore,
Save one, one only, when I stood forlorn,
Knowing my heart's best treasure was no more;
That neither present time, nor years unborn
Could to my sight that heavenly face restore.

William Wordsworth

7

"How can I save you from my own despair
To think I may not love you as before?"

Incantatory Poem

Hearing that you would come who by my love
Have dreamed me into your head these lost long days
I have caught birds and freed their essential blaze
For still I am as always my heart's hungering slave
And thus but dream life into its beat form
Singing up voices out of the wine-gay blood.

Water and wine being the elements
I was big with cliffs and water-wracking rocks
And huger than I my heart hearing your own
Racing thus to come nearest home with cloud
Under its rain-bearing leaves that were your name
Meaning waif of the tribe of cloud and rain,
Hearing that you would come, blood climbed on bone.

Hearing that you would come in the green cold days
Neither good nor great, my wine-flown blood
Got up incanting sleep's towers to the moon
To pray she bring her sailing presence round
From the back of night that she flag you home
(And dry brook beds she rushes into sound)
Lest all be storm-blown out to deeps
Raging beyond your name, and you not come
By spring's first fields already clad
To herald your long ride down.

By spring's first fields where the darkness there
Rose up to put your wild warmth on
Till absence shaped your body by absence learned
On the pitch of dark to light at my very hand

Under whose pulse you lay where my shaking heart
By its long stroke got you out of sleep
Into dream's childing origins.
Your name wearing water in cloud and flame
The world bearing flowers out of your name
Or in the dim sleep nothing borne
But the sound of waters racing your blood
And the running of waters and the dim
Bemused confession of waters foretelling your coming,

Bearing in morning over the threshold
South-infused, storm-centered, surly,
Purely peace-seeking as the rose
Till wonder lay waking at the heart early
Hearing that you would come for whom by my love
Bells and their tongues wait,
Birds in the bell of the bush their small songs halt.

Hearing that you would come
By the waters charged with your traveling home
On the speed of the surf-worked spume,
I make a prayer I shape upon a poem
Cut from the essential dealers of the green,
Too long dissembled from the water-swearing birds
And make a poem I shape upon a prayer
To this all-fathering dark now come to flower
When day has broken and we lie
Crossed with birds out of your name
I stole by watches of the griefless dream
In the element of the wine-transfiguring world.

                                        Jean Garrigue

The Garden of Love

I went to the Garden of Love,
And saw what I never had seen:
A Chapel was built in the midst,
Where I used to play on the green.

And the gates of this Chapel were shut,
And "Thou shalt not" writ over the door;
So I turn'd to the Garden of Love
That so many sweet flowers bore;

And I saw it was filled with graves,
And tomb-stones where flowers should be;
And Priests in black gowns were walking their rounds,
And binding with briars my joys & desires.

William Blake

"What thing is love?"

What thing is love? for (well I wot) love is a thing,
It is a prick, it is a sting,
It is a pretty, pretty thing;
It is a fire, it is a coal,
Whose flame creeps in at every hole;
And as my wit doth best devise,
Love's dwelling is in ladies' eyes,
From whence do glance love's piercing darts
That make such holes into our hearts;
And all the world herein accord
Love is a great and mighty lord;

And when he list to mount so high,
With Venus he in heaven doth lie,
And evermore hath been a god
Since Mars and she played even and odd.

George Peele

Sonnet XVIII: *"O kiss me yet again,* *O kiss me over"*

O kiss me yet again, O kiss me over
  And over! Kiss me this time tenderly;
  And this time let your passion enter me
  And burn me through! I shall return, my lover,
Four more for every one you give me—yes,
  Ten more if you desire it, still more tender.
  Dreamy and drugged with kisses we shall wander
  Through all our utter, intermingled bliss!
And so in each of us two lives have grown
  Concealed in one; our lover's, and our own.
  A paradox has gathered in my brain:
For while my life is disciplined and lonely,
  My heart is ill, and can recover only
  When it escapes, and breaks in two again.

Louise Labé
Translated from the French
by Frederic Prokosch

193

Among the Multitude

Among the men and women the multitude,
I perceive one picking me out by secret and divine signs,
Acknowledging none else, not parent, wife, husband, brother,
    child, any nearer than I am,
Some are baffled, but that one is not—that one knows me.

Ah, lover, and perfect equal,
I meant that you should discover me so by faint indirections,
And I when I meet you mean to discover you by the like in you.

Walt Whitman

Love

Love bade me welcome, yet my soul drew back,
    Guilty of dust and sin.
But quick-eyed Love, observing me grow slack
    From my first entrance in,
Drew nearer to me, sweetly questioning
    If I lacked anything.

A guest, I answered, worthy to be here.
    Love said, You shall be he.
I, the unkind, the ungrateful? ah, my dear,
    I cannot look on thee.
Love took my hand and smiling did reply,
    Who made the eyes but I?

Truth, Lord, but I have marred them; let my shame
    Go where it doth deserve.
And know you not, says Love, who bore the blame?
    My dear, then I will serve.
You must sit down, says Love, and taste my meat.
    So I did sit and eat.

George Herbert

Didymus

Refusing to fall in love with God, he gave
Himself to the love of created things,
Accepting only what he could see, a river
Full of the shadows of swallows' wings

That dipped and skimmed the water; he would not
Ask where the water ran or why.
When he died a swallow seemed to plunge
Into the reflected, the wrong sky.

Louis MacNeice

"Adam lay i-bowndyn"

Adam lay i-bowndyn,
   bowndyn in a bond,
Fowre thowsand wynter
   thowt he not to long;
And al was for an appil,
   an appil that he tok,
As clerkes fyndyn wretyn
   in here book.
Ne haddé the appil také ben
   the appil taken ben,
Ne haddé never our lady
   a ben hevené qwen.
Blyssid be the tyme
   that appil také was,
Therefore we mown syngyn
   Deo gracias.

Anonymous
(*From the Anglo-Saxon
and Middle English*)

"There is a Lady sweet and kind"

There is a Lady sweet and kind,
Was never face so pleased my mind;
I did but see her passing by,
And yet I love her till I die.

Her gesture, motion, and her smiles,
Her wit, her voice my heart beguiles,
Beguiles my heart, I know not why,
And yet I love her till I die.

Cupid is wingèd and doth range
Her country, so my love doth change:
But change she earth, or change she sky,
Yet will I love her till I die.

Thomas Ford

To His Coy Love

I pray thee leave, love me no more,
    Call home the heart you gave me!
I but in vain that saint adore
    That can but will not save me.
These poor half-kisses kill me quite;
    Was ever man thus servèd,
Amidst an ocean of delight,
    For pleasure to be starvèd?

Show me no more those snowy breasts
    With azure riverets branchèd,
Where, whilst mine eye with plenty feasts,
    Yet is my thirst not stanchèd.
O Tantalus, thy pains ne'er tell!
    By me thou art prevented:
'Tis nothing to be plagued in Hell,
    But thus in Heaven tormented!

Clip me no more in those dear arms,
    Nor thy life's comfort call me!
Oh, these are but too powerful charms,
    And do but more enthral me.
But see, how patient I am grown
    In all this coil about thee!
Come, nice thing, let thy heart alone!
    I cannot live without thee.

Michael Drayton

Song

Sylvia the fair, in the bloom of fifteen,
Felt an innocent warmth as she lay on the green;
She had heard of a pleasure, and something she guessed
By the towsing and tumbling and touching her breast;
She saw the men eager, but was at a loss
What they meant by their sighing and kissing so close;
        By their praying and whining,
        And clasping and twining,
        And panting and wishing,
        And sighing and kissing,
        And sighing and kissing so close.

Ah, she cried, ah, for a languishing maid
In a country of Christians to die without aid.
Not a Whig or a Tory or Trimmer at least,
Or a Protestant parson or Catholic priest,
To instruct a young virgin that is at a loss
What they meant by their sighing and kissing so close;
        By their praying &c.

Cupid in shape of a swain did appear;
He saw the sad wound, and in pity drew near,
Then showed her his arrow and bid her not fear,
For the pain was no more than a maiden may bear;
When the balm was infused, she was not at a loss
What they meant by their sighing and kissing so close;
     By their praying &c.

John Dryden

A *Lost Jewel*

Who on your breast pillows his head now,
Jubilant to have won
The heart beneath on fire for him alone,

At dawn will hear you, plagued by nightmare,
Mumble and weep
About some blue jewel you were sworn to keep.

Wake, blink, laugh out in reassurance,
Yet your tears will say.
'It was not mine to lose or give away.

'For love it shone—never for the madness
Of a strange bed—
Light on my finger, fortune in my head.'

Roused by your naked grief and beauty,
For lust he will burn:
'Turn to me, sweetheart! Why do you not turn?'

Robert Graves

The Racetrack

Under our stillness fled the same low hooves—
After, before, from the first morning when
We stood to watch the horses exercise.
Like a small sea the track dazzled our eyes:
Two riders shouting, flattening to run,
A spray of turf flung glistening toward the sun,
Stallions and fillies combing like distant waves.

Blind, pounding beasts came whirling through the mist,
Sweat on their flanks, their ankles wreathed in spume,
The day I told you of my loneliness;
Or I saw darkly out of such distress
As knocked my heart against its fragile room
Until our eyes touched and that light went home—
So we were one before we spoke or kissed.

Now that our bodies move and wake as one
That daybreak dream of horses has changed too
And we are free to say, as shadows scatter,
"Sound carries on this track as on deep water."
The trees shake out their leaves. We feel the slow
Rotation of a world in which we grow;
Slowly we learn our long wave's luminous motion.

Jane Cooper

Fiametta

Fiametta walks under the quincebuds
    In a gown the color of flowers;
Her small breasts shine through the silken stuff
    Like raindrops after showers.
The green hem of her dress is silk, but duller
Than her eye's green color.

Her shadow restores the grass's green—
    Where the sun had gilded it;
The air has given her copper hair
    The sanguine that was requisite.
Whatever her flaws, my lady
Has no fault in her young body.

She leans with her long slender arms
    To pull down morning upon her—
Fragrance of quince, white light and falling cloud.
    The day shall have lacked due honor
Until I shall have rightly praised
Her standing thus with slight arms upraised.

John Peale Bishop

Evadne

I first tasted under Apollo's lips,
love and love sweetness,
I, Evadne;
my hair is made of crisp violets

or hyacinth which the wind combs back
across some rock shelf;
I, Evadne,
was mate of the god of light.

His hair was crisp to my mouth,
as the flower of the crocus,
across my cheek,
cool as the silver-cress
on Erotos bank;
between my chin and throat,
his mouth slipped over and over.

Still between my arm and shoulder,
I feel the brush of his hair,
and my hands keep the gold they took,
as they wandered over and over,
that great arm-full of yellow flowers.

H.D.

. . . I wrote a Letter for you yesterday expecting to have seen your mother. I shall be selfish enough to send it though I know it may give you a little pain, because I wish you to see how unhappy I am for love of you, and endeavour as much as I can to entice you to give up your whole heart to me whose whole existence hangs upon you. You could not step or move an eyelid but it would shoot to my heart—I am greedy of you—Do not think of any thing but me. Do not live as if I was not existing—Do not forget me—But have I any right to say you forget me? Perhaps you think of me all day. Have I any right to wish you to be unhappy for me? You would forgive me for wishing it, if you knew the extreme passion I have that you should love me—and for you to love me as I do you, you must think of no one but me, much less write that sentence. Yesterday and this morning I have been haunted with a sweet vision—I have seen you the whole time in your shepherdess dress. How my senses have ached at it! How my heart has been devoted to it! How my eyes have been full of Tears at it! I[n]deed I think a real Love is enough to occupy the widest heart . . . Well may you exclaim, how selfish, how cruel, not to let me enjoy my youth! to wish me to be unhappy!

You must be so if you love me—upon my Soul I can be contented with nothing else. If you could really what is call'd enjoy yourself at a Party—if you can smile in peoples faces, and wish them to admire you *now*, you never have nor ever will love me—I see *life* in nothing but the cerrtainty of your Love—convince me of it my sweetest. If I am not somehow convinc'd I shall die of agony. If we love we must not live as other men and women do—I cannot brook the wolfsbane of fashion and foppery and tattle. You must be mine to die upon the rack if I want you. I do not pretend to say I have more feeling than my fellows—but I wish you seriously to look over my letters kind and unkind and consider whether the Person who wrote them can be able to endure much longer the agonies and uncertainties which you are so peculiarly

made to create—My recovery of bodily hea[l]th will be of no
benefit to me if you are not all mine when I am well. For god's
sake save me—or tell me my passion is of too awful a nature for
you. Again God bless you

J.K.

No—my sweet Fanny—I am wrong. I do not want you to be un-
happy—and yet I do, I must while there is so sweet a Beauty—
my loveliest my darling! Good bye! I kiss you—O the tor-
ments! . . .

*Letter from John Keats
to Fanny Brawne, May* 1820.

204

Poetry

I recognized you because when I saw the print
Of your foot on the pathway
My heart hurt when you trod upon me.
I ran madly; I went seeking all day long
Like a dog without a master.
You were gone already! And your foot was treading
On my heart, in an endless flight
As if this were the roadway
That carried you off forever . . .

Juan Ramón Jiménez

"As you came from the holy land of Walsingham"

As you came from the holy land
　　Of Walsingham,
Met you not with my true love,
　　By the way as you came?

How shall I know your true love,
　　That have met many one
As I went to the holy land,
　　That have come, that have gone?

She is neither white nor brown,
　　But as the heavens fair;
There is none hath her form so divine,
　　In the earth, or the air.

Such an one did I meet, good sir,
    Such an angelic face,
Who like a queen, like a nymph, did appear
    By her gait, by her grace.

She hath left me here alone,
    All alone as unknown,
Who sometime did me lead with herself,
    And me loved as her own.

What's the cause that she leaves you alone,
    And a new way doth take,
Who loved you once as her own,
    And her joy did you make?

I have loved her all my youth,
    But now old, as you see,
Love likes not the falling fruit
    From the withered tree.

Know that love is a careless child,
    And forgets promise past;
He is blind, he is deaf, when he list,
    And in faith never fast.

His desire is a dureless content,
    And a trustless joy;
He is won with a world of despair,
    And is lost with a toy.

Of women-kind such indeed is the love,
    Or the word, love, abused,
Under which many childish desires
    And conceits are excused.

But true love is a durable fire
   In the mind ever burning,
Never sick, never old, never dead
   From itself never turning.

Sir Walter Raleigh

"My darling dear, my daisy flower"

With lullay, lullay, like a child,
Thou sleepest too long, thou art beguiled.

My darling dear, my daisy flower,
   Let me, quod he, lie in your lap.
Lie still, quod she, my paramour,
   Lie still hardely, and take a nap.
   His head was heavy, such was his hap,
All drowsy dreaming, drowned in sleep,
That of his love he took no keep.
   With hey lullay, lullay, like a child,
   Thou sleepest too long, thou art beguiled.

With ba, ba, ba! and bas, bas, bas!
   She cherished him both cheek and chin,
That he wist never where he was:
   He had forgotten all deadly sin.
   He wanted wit her love to win:
He trusted her payment and lost all his pay;
She left him sleeping and stole away.
   With hey lullay, lullay, like a child,
   Thou sleepest too long, thou art beguiled.

The rivers rough, the waters wan,
    She sparèd not to wet her feet;
She waded over, she found a man
    That halsèd her heartily and kissed her sweet:
    Thus after her cold she caught a heat.
My love, she said, routeth in his bed;
Ywis he hath an heavy head.
    With hey lullay, lullay, like a child,
    Thou sleepest too long, thou art beguiled.

What dreamest thou, drunkard, drowsy pate?
    Thy lust and liking is from thee gone;
Thou blinkard blowbowl, thou wakest too late,
    Behold thou liest, luggard, alone!
    Well may thou sigh, well may thou groan,
To deal with her so cowardly:
Ywis, pole hatchet, she bleared thine eye.

John Skelton

"I found her out there"

I found her out there
On a slope few see,
That falls westwardly
To the salt-edged air,
Where the ocean breaks
On the purple strand,
And the hurricane shakes
The solid land.

I brought her here,
And have laid her to rest
In a noiseless nest
No sea beats near.
She will never be stirred
In her loamy cell
By the waves long heard
And loved so well.

So she does not sleep
By those haunted heights
The Atlantic smites
And the blind gales sweep,
Whence she often would gaze
At Dundagel's famed head,
While the dipping blaze
Dyed her face fire-red;

And would sigh at the tale
Of sunk Lyonnesse,
As a wind-tugged tress
Flapped her cheek like a flail;
Or listen at whiles
With a thought-bound brow
To the murmuring miles
She is far from now.

Yet her shade, maybe,
Will creep underground
Till it catch the sound
Of that western sea
As it swells and sobs
Where she once domiciled,
And joy in its throbs
With the heart of a child.

Thomas Hardy

Poem to the Mysterious Woman

I have dreamed so much of you
that you lose your reality
Is there still time to reach that living body
  and kiss on that mouth the birth
  of the voice which is dear to me.
I have dreamed so much of you
that my arms accustomed while embracing your shadow
  to folding over my breast would not bend
  to the shape of your body perhaps.
And that, before the real appearance of what has haunted me
  and ruled me for days and years
I should become doubtless a shade,
O sentimental scales
I have dreamed of you so much that it is no longer right
  for me to awaken. I sleep standing my body exposed to
  all the appearances of life and love, and you, the only
  one who counts today for me, I could touch your brow
  and your lips less
than the lips and brow of the first person who came.
I have dreamed so much of you
walked so much, spoken, lain with your phantom that all
  I have to do now perhaps is to be a phantom among
  phantoms and a ghost a hundred times more than the
  ghost who walks and will walk gaily over the sun-dial
  of your life.

       Robert Desnos
       Translated from the French
       by Wallace Fowlie

The Vision to Electra

I Dream'd we both were in a bed
Of Roses, almost smothered:
The warmth and sweetnes had me there
Made lovingly familiar:
But that I heard thy sweet breath say,
Faults done by night, will blush by day:
I kist thee (panting) and I call
Night to the Record! that was all.
But ah! if empty dreames so please,
Love give me more such nights as these.

Robert Herrick

Semele to Jupiter

With my frailty, don't upbraid me,
     I am woman as you made me;
Causeless doubting, or despairing,
Rashly trusting, idly fearing:
     If obtaining,
     Still complaining;
     If consenting,
     Still repenting;
     Most complying,
     Then denying:
And to be followed, only flying.

With my frailty, don't upbraid me:
I am woman as you made me.

William Congreve

Astrophel and Stella 59:
"Dear, why make you more of
a dog than me?"

Dear, why make you more of a dog than me?
    If he do love, I burn, I burn in love;
    If he wait well, I never thence would move;
    If he be fair, yet but a dog can be.
Little he is, so little worth is he;
    He barks, my songs thine own voice oft doth prove;
    Bidden, perhaps he fetcheth thee a glove,
    But I unbid, fetch even my soul to thee.
Yet while I languish, him that bosom clips,
    That lap doth lap, nay lets, in spite of spite,
    This sour-breathed mate taste of those sug'red lips.
Alas, if you grant only such delight
    To witless things, then Love I hope (since wit
    Becomes a clog) will soon ease me of it.

Sir Philip Sidney

River-Mates

I'll be an otter, and I'll let you swim
A mate beside me; we will venture down
A deep, dark river, when the sky above
Is shut of the sun; spoilers are we,
Thick-coated; no dog's tooth can bite at our veins,
With eyes and ears of poachers; deep-earthed ones
Turned hunters; let him slip past
The little vole; my teeth are on an edge
For the King-fish of the River!

        I hold him up
The glittering salmon that smells of the sea;
I hold him high and whistle!
        Now we go
Back to our earths; we will tear and eat
Sea-smelling salmon; you will tell the cubs
I am the Booty-bringer, I am the Lord
Of the River; the deep, dark, full and flowing River!

                              Padraic Colum

To A.D.

The nightingale has a lyre of gold,
    The lark's is a clarion call,
And the blackbird plays but a boxwood flute,
    But I love him best of all.

For his song is all of the joy of life,
    And we in the mad, spring weather,
We two have listened till he sang
    Our hearts and lips together.

                        William Ernest Henley

Ode VIII: *"In the name of all the gods, tell me, Lydia, why"*

In the name of all the gods, tell me, Lydia, why
thou art bent on ruining Sybaris with love; why he
hates the sunny Campus, he who once was patient of
the dust and sun; why he rides no more among his

213

soldier mates, nor restrains the mouth of his Gallic
steed with jagged bit! Why does he fear to touch
the yellow Tiber? Why does he shun the wrestling-oil
more warily than viper's blood, nor longer show his
arms bruised with weapon practice, he who once was
famed for hurling, oft the discus, oft the javelin,
beyond the farthest mark? Why does he skulk, as
they say the son of sea-born Thetis did, when the
time of Troy's fearful destruction drew near, for fear
that the garb of men should hurry him to slaughter
and the Lycian bands?

Horace
*Translated from the Latin
by C. E. Bennett*

From The Princess 3:
"*Now sleeps the crimson petal,
now the white*"

Now sleeps the crimson petal, now the white;
Nor waves the cypress in the palace walk;
Nor winks the gold fin in the porphyry font.
The fire-fly wakens; waken thou with me.

Now droops the milk-white peacock like a ghost,
And like a ghost she glimmers on to me.

Now lies the Earth all Danaë to the stars,
And all thy heart lies open unto me.

214

Now slides the silent meteor on, and leaves
A shining furrow, as thy thoughts in me.

Now folds the lily all her sweetness up,
And slips into the bosom of the lake.
So fold thyself, my dearest, thou, and slip
Into my bosom and be lost in me.

Alfred Tennyson

Song: *"Nymphs and shepherds dance no more"*

Nymphs and shepherds dance no more
By sandy *Ladons* Lillied banks,
On old *Lycaeus* or *Cyllene* hoar,
   Trip no more in twilight ranks,
Though *Erymanth* your loss deplore,
   A better soyl shall give ye thanks.
From the stony *Maenalus*,
Bring your Flocks, and live with us,
Here ye shall have greater grace,
To serve the Lady of this place.
   Though *Syrinx* your *Pans* Mistress were,
   Yet *Syrinx* well might wait on her.
     Such a rural Queen
  All *Arcadia* hath not seen.

John Milton

Sonnet: *"I must not grieve my love, whose eyes would read"*

I must not grieve my love, whose eyes would read
Lines of delight, whereon her youth might smile.
Flowers have time before they come to seed,
And she is young, and now must sport the while.
And sport, Sweet Maid, in season of these years
And learn to gather flowers before they wither;
And where the sweetest blossom first appears,
Let Love and Youth conduct thy pleasures thither,
Lighten forth smiles to clear the clouded air,
And calm the tempest which my sighs do raise;
Pity and smiles do best become the fair;
Pity and smiles must only yield thee praise.
Make me to say, when all my griefs are gone,
Happy the heart that sighed for such a one.

Samuel Daniel

"If thou must love me, let it be for nought"

If thou must love me, let it be for nought
Except for love's sake only. Do not say
'I love her for her smile—her look—her way
Of speaking gently,—for a trick of thought
That falls in well with mine, and certes brought
A sense of pleasant ease on such a day'—
For these things in themselves, Belovèd, may
Be changed, or change for thee,—and love, so wrought,
May be unwrought so. Neither love me for
Thine own dear pity's wiping my cheeks dry,—

216

A creature might forget to weep, who bore
Thy comfort long, and lose thy love thereby!
But love me for love's sake, that evermore
Thou mayst love on, through love's eternity.

Elizabeth Barrett Browning

"First time he kissed me,
he but only kissed"

First time he kissed me, he but only kissed
The fingers of this hand wherewith I write;
And ever since, it grew more clean and white,
Slow to world-greetings, quick with its 'Oh, list,'
When the angels speak. A ring of amethyst
I could not wear here, plainer to my sight,
Than that first kiss. The second passed in height
The first, and sought the forehead, and half missed,
Half falling on the hair. O beyond meed!
That was the chrism of love, which love's own crown,
With sanctifying sweetness, did precede.
The third upon my lips was folded down
In perfect, purple state; since when, indeed,
I have been proud and said, 'My love, my own.'

Elizabeth Barrett Browning

Ode to Anactoria

Peer of the golden gods is he to Sappho,
He, the happy man who sits beside thee,
Heark'ning so divinely close thy lovely
        Speech and dear laughter.

This it was that made to flutter wildly
Heart of mine in bosom panting wildly! . . .
Oh! I need to see thee but a little,
    When, as at lightning,

Voice within me stumbles, tongue is broken,
Tingles all my flesh with subtle fire,
Ring my ears with waterfalls and thunders,
    Eyes are in midnight,

And a sweat bedews me like a shower,
Tremor hunts my body down and seizes,
Till, as one about to die, I linger
    Paler than grass is. . . .

                        Sappho
                        *Translated from the Greek
                        by William Ellery Leonard*

Beeny Cliff

I

O the opal and the sapphire of that wandering western sea,
And the woman riding high above with bright hair flapping
    free—
The woman whom I loved so, and who loyally loved me.

II

The pale mews plained below us, and the waves seemed far away
In a nether sky, engrossed in saying their ceaseless babbling say,
As we laughed light-heartedly aloft on that clear-sunned March
    day.

III

A little cloud then cloaked us, and there flew an irised rain,
And the Atlantic dyed its levels with a dull misfeatured stain,
And then the sun burst out again, and purples prinked the main.

IV

—Still in all its chasmal beauty bulks old Beeny to the sky,
And shall she and I not go there once again now March is nigh,
And the sweet things said in that March say anew there by and
    by?

V

What if still in chasmal beauty looms that wild weird western
    shore,
The woman now is—elsewhere—whom the ambling pony bore,
And nor knows nor cares for Beeny, and will laugh there never-
    more.

Thomas Hardy

The Spouting Horn

I stood by the stone sea-wall at Depoe Bay
And watched that slowly quickening rage of waves
At high tide, with my son and one-year daughter.
Each elemental seventh, ramming in
Sent the sea's tumult through the spouting horn,
A natural fissure in the heaps of basalt:
A stream shot skyward like a waterfall,
A Helicon that rode the wet horizon.

219

Love's witnesses looked back at Genesis:
The winged horse stamped on the basalt cliff:
Soul and sense spouted in the light
As when the Whirlwind spoke to Job's desire
The sensual particulars of Awe.
"Let the floods clap their hands," the Psalmist wrote.
I praised by the sea-wall, having been given
Poems and children, the holiest shapes of love.

Nelson Bentley

A Complaint by Night
of the Lover Not Beloved

Alas, so all things now do hold their peace!
   Heaven and earth disturbèd in no thing;
The beasts, the air, the birds their song do cease,
   The nightès car the stars about doth bring;
Calm is the sea; the waves work less and less:
   So am not I, whom love, alas! doth wring,
Bringing before my face the great increase
   Of my desires, whereat I weep and sing,
In joy and woe, as in a doubtful case.
   For my sweet thoughts sometime do pleasure bring;
But by and by, the cause of my disease
   Gives me a pang that inwardly doth sting,
When that I think what grief it is again
To live and lack the thing should rid my pain.

Francesco Petrarca
Translated from the Italian
by Henry Howard, Earl of Surrey

On My First Son

Farewell, thou child of my right hand, and joy,
My sin was too much hope of thee, loved boy:
Seven years th' wert lent to me, and I thee pay,
Exacted by thy fate, on the just day.
O, I could lose all father now. For why
Will man lament the state he should envy?
To have so soon 'scaped world's and flesh's rage,
And, if no other misery, yet age?
Rest in soft peace, and, asked, say here doth lie
Ben Jonson his best piece of poetry:
For whose sake, henceforth, all his vows be such
As what he loves may never like too much.

Ben Jonson

The Starred Coverlet

A difficult achievement for true lovers
Is to lie mute, without embrace or kiss,
Without a rustle or a smothered sigh,
Basking each in the other's glory.

Let us not undervalue lips or arms
As reassurances of constancy,
Or speech as necessary communication
When troubled hearts go groping through the dusk;

Yet lovers who have learned this last refinement—
To lie apart, yet sleep and dream together
Motionless under their starred coverlet—
Crown love with wreaths of myrtle.

Robert Graves

"They flee from me that sometime did me seek"

They flee from me that sometime did me seek,
  With naked foot stalking in my chamber:
I have seen them gentle, tame, and meek,
  That now are wild, and do not once remember
  That sometime they have put themselves in danger
To take bread at my hand: and now they range,
Busily seeking with a continual change.

Thanked be fortune, it hath been otherwise
  Twenty times better; but once, in special,
In thin array, after a pleasant guise,
  When her loose gown from her shoulders did fall,
  And she me caught in her arms long and small,
Therewith all sweetly did me kiss,
And softly said, *'Dear heart, how like you this?'*

It was no dream; I lay broad waking:
  But all is turned, thorough my gentleness,
Into a strange fashion of forsaking;
  And I have leave to go, of her goodness;
  And she also to use new-fangleness.
But since that I so unkindly am served,
I fain would know what she hath deserved.

Sir Thomas Wyatt

8

"And yet we were what we are.
And though the smoke is gone
        there is some fire
In saying so."

Modern Love

And what is love? It is a doll dress'd up
For idleness to cosset, nurse, and dandle;
A thing of soft misnomers, so divine
That silly youth doth think to make itself
Divine by loving, and so goes on
Yawning and doting a whole summer long,
Till Miss's comb is made a pearl tiara,
And common Wellingtons turn Romeo boots;
Then Cleopatra lives at number seven,
And Antony resides in Brunswick Square.
Fools! if some passions high have warm'd the world,
If Queens and Soldiers have play'd deep for hearts,
It is no reason why such agonies
Should be more common than the growth of weeds.
Fools! make me whole again that weighty pearl
The Queen of Egypt melted, and I'll say
That ye may love in spite of beaver hats.

John Keats

Caryatid

Not at midnight, not at morning, O sweet city,
Shall we come in at your portal, but this girl,
Bearing on her head a broken stone,
In the body shaped to this, the throat and bosom
Poised no less for the burden now the temple is fallen,
Tells the white Athenian wonder overthrown.

There is no clasp which stays beauty forever.
Time has undone her, from porphyry, from bronze.
She is winged every way and will not rest;
But the gesture of the lover shall remain long after,
Where lovely and imponderable there leans
A weight more grave than marble on the breast.

Léonie Adams

Western Winde

Western winde, when will thou blow,
The smalle raine downe can raine?
Christ if my love were in my armes,
And I in my bed againe.

Anonymous

The Dream of a Lover

Benedicite! whate dreamed I this nyght?
Methought the worlde was turnyd up so downe
The sun, the moone had lost their force and lyght,
The sea also drowned both toure and towne.
Yet more marvel how that I heard the sounde
Of onys voyce saying: beare in thy mynd,
Thi lady hath forgotten to be kynd.

Anonymous

The Folly of Being Comforted

One that is ever kind said yesterday:
'Your well-beloved's hair has threads of gray,
And little shadows come about her eyes;
Time can but make it easier to be wise
Though now it seems impossible, and so
All that you need is patience.'
                        Heart cries, 'No,
I have not a crumb of comfort, not a grain.
Time can but make her beauty over again:
Because of that great nobleness of hers
The fire that stirs about her, when she stirs,
Burns but more clearly. O she had not these ways
When all the wild summer was in her gaze.'

O heart! O heart! if she'd but turn her head,
You'd know the folly of being comforted.

                                        W. B. Yeats

"Why art thou silent! Is thy love a plant"

Why art thou silent! Is thy love a plant
Of such weak fibre that the treacherous air
Of absence withers what was once so fair?
Is there no debt to pay, no boon to grant?
Yet have my thoughts for thee been vigilant—
Bound to thy service with unceasing care,
The mind's least generous wish a mendicant

228

For nought but what thy happiness could spare.
Speak—though this soft warm heart, once free to hold
A thousand tender pleasures, thine and mine,
Be left more desolate, more dreary cold
Than a forsaken bird's-nest filled with snow
'Mid its own bush of leafless eglantine—
Speak, that my torturing doubts their end may know.

William Wordsworth

Ballad of Love and Blood

As on a dark guitar,
I played your naked body;
your tresses were ribbons,
black ribbons, but not of mourning.

With teeth of clear moonlight
I bit the song's ripe fruit;
we lay drenched in the milky
shadows of the moon.

Your cry winged the night—
arrow of bloodwet gold:—
Ai, ai, ai, it was the song
that pleased me so!

Black ribbons were your tresses,
black ribbons, but not of mourning;
in my hand the jasmines
of your complaint and pleasure.

Ah little dusky girl
in the shadowy fringes
of woven song and sorrow,
white moon and scented sweetness!

Your tresses were ribbons,
black ribbons, but not of mourning!

Angel Miguel Queremel
*Translated from the Spanish
by Rolfe Humphries*

"Strange fits of passion have I known"

Strange fits of passion have I known:
And I will dare to tell,
But in the Lover's ear alone,
What once to me befell.

When she I loved looked every day
Fresh as a rose in June,
I to her cottage bent my way,
Beneath an evening-moon.

Upon the moon I fixed my eye,
All over the wide lea;
With quickening pace my horse drew nigh
Those paths so dear to me.

And now we reached the orchard plot;
And, as we climbed the hill,
The sinking moon to Lucy's cot
Came near, and nearer still.

In one of those sweet dreams I slept,
Kind Nature's gentlest boon!
And all the while my eyes I kept
On the descending moon.

My horse moved on; hoof after hoof
He raised, and never stopped:
When down behind the cottage roof,
At once, the bright moon dropped.

What fond and wayward thoughts will slide
Into a Lover's head!
"O mercy!" to myself I cried,
"If Lucy should be dead!"

William Wordsworth

"Dear, if you change"

Dear, if you change, I'll never choose again;
Sweet, if you shrink, I'll never think of love;
Fair, if you fail, I'll judge all beauty vain;
Wise, if too weak, more wits I'll never prove.
Dear, sweet, fair, wise,—change, shrink, nor be not weak;
And on my faith, my faith shall never break.

Earth with her flowers shall sooner heaven adorn;
Heaven her bright stars through earth's dim globe shall move;
Fire heat shall lose, and frosts of flame be born;
Air, made to shine, as black as hell shall prove:
Earth, heaven, fire, air, the world transformed shall view,
Ere I prove false to faith, or strange to you.

John Dowland

Cy Est Pourtraicte, Madame
Ste. Ursule, Et Les Unze
Mille Vierges

Ursula, in a garden, found
A bed of radishes.
She kneeled upon the ground
And gathered them,
With flowers around,
Blue, gold, pink, and green.

She dressed in red and gold brocade
And in the grass an offering made
Of radishes and flowers.

She said, "My dear,
Upon your altars,
I have placed
The marguerite and coquelicot,
And roses
Frail as April snow;
"But here," she said,
"Where none can see,
I make an offering, in the grass,
Of radishes and flowers."
And then she wept
For fear the Lord would not accept.
The good Lord in his Garden sought
New leaf and shadowy tinct,
And they were all His thought.
He heard her low accord,
Half prayer and half ditty,

And He felt a subtle quiver,
That was not heavenly love,
Or pity.

This is not writ
In any book.

Wallace Stevens

"When thou must home"

When thou must home to shades of underground,
And there arrived, a new admired guest,
The beauteous spirits do ingirt thee round,
White Iope, blithe Helen, and the rest,
To hear the stories of thy finished love
From that smooth tongue whose music hell can move;

Then wilt thou speak of banqueting delights,
Of masks and revels which sweet youth did make,
Of tourneys and great challenges of knights,
And all these triumphs for thy beauties' sake:
When thou hast told these honors done to thee,
Then tell, O tell, how thou didst murder me.

Sextus Aurelius Propertius
Translated from the Latin
by Thomas Campion

"If no love is, O God, what fele I so?"

If no love is, O God, what fele I so?
    And if love is, what thing and which is he?
    If love be good, from whennes cometh my woo?
    If it be wikke, a wonder thynketh me,
    When every torment and adversite
    That cometh of hym, may to me savory thinke,
    For ay thurst I, the more that ich it drynke.
And if that at myn owen lust I brenne,
    From whennes cometh my waillynge and my pleynte?
    If harm agree me, whereto pleyne I thenne?
    I noot, ne whi unwery that I feynte.
    O quike deth, O swete harm so queynte,
    How may of the in me swich quantite,
    But if that I consente that it be?
And if that I consente, I wrongfully
    Compleyne, iwis. Thus possed to and fro,
    Al sterelees withinne a boot am I
    Amydde the see, betwixen wyndes two,
    That in contrarie stonden evere mo.
    Allas! what is this wondre maladie?
    For hete of cold, for cold of hete, I dye.

Francesco Petrarca
*Translated from the Italian
by Geoffrey Chaucer*

The Language

Locate *I*
love you some-
where in

teeth and
eyes, bite
it but

take care not
to hurt, you
want so

much so
little. Words
say everything,

I
love you
again,

then what
is emptiness
for. To

fill, fill.
I heard words
and words full

of holes
aching. Speech
is a mouth.

Robert Creeley

235

Twice of the Same Fever

No one can die twice of the same fever?
   Tell them it is untrue:
Have we not died three deaths, and three again,
   You of me, I of you?

The chill, the frantic pulse, brows burning,
   Lips broken by thirst—
Until, in darkness, a ghost grieves:
   'It was I died the first.'

Worse than such death, even is resurrection.
   Do we dare laugh away
Disaster, and with a callous madrigal
   Salute the new day?

Robert Graves

Love's Good-Morrow

Pack, clouds, away! and welcome day!
   With night we banish sorrow;
Sweet air, blow soft, mount larks aloft
   To give my love good-morrow!
Wings from the wind to please her mind,
   Notes from the lark I'll borrow;
Bird, prune thy wing, nightingale, sing,
   To give my love good-morrow;
   To give my love good-morrow,
   Notes from them both I'll borrow.

236

Wake from thy nest, Robin Redbreast,
  Sing birds in every furrow;
And from each hill, let music shrill
  Give my fair love good-morrow!
Blackbird and thrush in every bush,
    Stare, linnet, and cock-sparrow!
You pretty elves, amongst yourselves,
    Sing my fair love good-morrow;
    To give my love good-morrow,
    Sing birds in every furrow.

                    Thomas Heywood

Her Reticence

If I could send him only
One sleeve with my hand in it,
Disembodied, unbloody,
For him to kiss or caress
As he would or would not,—
But never the full look of my eyes,
Nor the whole heart of my thought,
Nor the soul haunting my body,
Nor my lips, my breasts, my thighs
That shiver in the wind
When the wind sighs.

                    Theodore Roethke

To His Coy Mistress

Had we but world enough and time,
This coyness, lady, were no crime.
We would sit down, and think which way
To walk, and pass our long love's day.
Thou by the Indian Ganges' side
Should'st rubies find; I by the tide
Of Humber would complain. I would
Love you ten years before the flood;
And you should if you please refuse
Till the conversion of the Jews.
My vegetable love should grow
Vaster than empires and more slow.
A hundred years should go to praise
Thine eyes, and on thy forehead gaze.
Two hundred to adore each breast;
But thirty thousand to the rest.
An age at least to every part,
And the last age should show your heart.
For, lady, you deserve this state,
Nor would I love at lower rate.
    But at my back I always hear
Time's wingèd chariot hurrying near;
And yonder all before us lie
Deserts of vast eternity.
Thy beauty shall no more be found,
Nor in thy marble vault shall sound
My echoing song; then worms shall try
That long preserved virginity,
And your quaint honour turn to dust,
And into ashes all my lust.
The grave's a fine and private place,
But none I think do there embrace.

Now therefore while the youthful hue
Sits on thy skin like morning dew,
And while thy willing soul transpires
At every pore with instant fires,
Now let us sport us while we may;
And now like amorous birds of prey
Rather at once our time devour
Than languish in his slow-chapped power.
Let us roll all our strength and all
Our sweetness up into one ball,
And tear our pleasures with rough strife
Thorough the iron gates of life.
Thus, though we cannot make our sun
Stand still, yet we will make him run.

                                    Andrew Marvell

Sweetest Fanny,

You fear, sometimes, I do not love you so much as you wish? My dear Girl I love you ever and ever and without reserve. The more I have known you the more have I lov'd. In every way— even my jealousies have been agonies of Love, in the hottest fit I ever had I would have died for you. I have vex'd you too much. But for Love! Can I help it? You are always new. The last of your kisses was ever the sweetest; the last smile the brightest; the last movement the gracefullest. When you pass'd my window home yesterday, I was fill'd with as much admiration as if I had then seen you for the first time. You uttered a half complaint once that I only lov'd your Beauty. Have I nothing else then to love in you but that? Do not I see a heart naturally furnish'd with wings imprison itself with me? No ill prospect has been able to turn your thoughts a moment from me. This perhaps should be as much a subject of sorrow as joy—but I will not talk of that. Even if you did not love me I could not help an entire devotion to you: how much more deeply then must I feel for you knowing you love me. My Mind has been the most discontented and restless one that ever was put into a body too small for it. I never felt my Mind repose upon anything with complete and undistracted enjoyment—upon no person but you. When you are in the room my thoughts never fly out of window: you always concentrate my whole senses. The anxiety shown about our Loves in your last note is an immense pleasure to me: however you must not suffer such speculations to molest you any more: nor will I any more believe you can have the least pique against me. . . .

Letter from John Keats
to Fanny Brawne, March 1820.

From Song of Myself: *"Twenty-eight young men bathe by the shore"*

Twenty-eight young men bathe by the shore;
Twenty-eight young men, and all so friendly:
Twenty-eight years of womanly life, and all so lonesome.

She owns the fine house by the rise of the bank;
She hides, handsome and richly drest, aft the blinds of the
    window.

Which of the young men does she like the best?
Ah, the homeliest of them is beautiful to her.
Where are you off to, lady? for I see you;
You splash in the water there, yet stay stock still in your room.

Dancing and laughing along the beach came the twenty-ninth
    bather;
The rest did not see her, but she saw them and loved them.

The beards of the young men glisten'd with wet, it ran from their
    long hair:
Little streams pass'd all over their bodies.

An unseen hand also pass'd over their bodies,
It descended tremblingly from their temples and ribs.

The young men float on their backs—their white bellies bulge to
    the sun—they do not ask who seizes fast to them;
They do not know who puffs and declines with pendant and bend-
    ing arch;
They do not think whom they souse with spray.

Walt Whitman

At the Wedding March

God with honour hang your head,
Groom, and grace you, bride, your bed
With lissome scions, sweet scions,
Out of hallowed bodies bred.

Each be other's comfort kind:
Déep, déeper than divined,
Divine charity, dear charity,
Fast you ever, fast bind.

Then let the march tread our ears:
I to him turn with tears
Who to wedlock, his wonder wedlock,
Déals tríumph and immortal years.

Gerard Manley Hopkins

"Call it a good marriage"

Call it a good marriage—
For no one ever questioned
Her warmth, his masculinity,
Their interlocking views;
Except one stray graphologist
Who frowned in speculation
At her h's and her s's
His p's and w's.

242

Though few would still subscribe
To the monogamic axiom
That strife below the hip-bones
Need not estrange the heart,
Call it a good marriage:
More drew those two together,
Despite a lack of children,
Than pulled them apart.

Call it a good marriage:
They never fought in public,
They acted circumspectly
And faced the world with pride;
Thus the hazards of their love-bed
Were none of our damned business—
Till as jurymen we sat on
Two deaths by suicide.

Robert Graves

With Child

Now I am slow and placid, fond of sun,
Like a sleek beast, or a worn one:
No slim and languid girl—not glad
With the windy trip I once had,

But velvet-footed, musing of my own,
Torpid, mellow, stupid as a stone.

You cleft me with your beauty's pulse, and now
Your pulse has taken body. Care not how
The old grace goes, how heavy I am grown,
Big with this loneliness, how you alone

243

Ponder our love. Touch my feet and feel
How earth tingles, teeming at my heel!
Earth's urge, not mine—my little death, not hers;
And the pure beauty yearns and stirs.

It does not heed our ecstasies, it turns
With secrets of its own, its own concerns,
Toward a windy world of its own, toward stark
And solitary places. In the dark,
Defiant even now, it tugs and moans
To be untangled from these mother's bones.

Genevieve Taggard

A *Pity*.
We Were Such a Good Invention

They amputated
Your thighs off my hips.
As far as I'm concerned
They are all surgeons. All of them.

They dismantled us
Each from the other.
As far as I'm concerned
They are all engineers. All of them.

A pity. We were such a good
And loving invention.
An airplane made from a man and wife.
Wings and everything.
We hovered a little above the earth.

We even flew a little.

Yehuda Amichai
*Translated from the Hebrew
by Assia Gutmann*

244

The Birthing

But she had seen the cattle drop their young,
their matted hairy flanks soaked with sweat,
bony legs shaking. Their milky eyes sought hers,
a swirl of color, of dumb question. Into the dung
and the saw of heavy breaths, blind and wet,
the calves somersaulted, head over heels,
skinny arms and legs crumpled together.
They lay against the cows' warm, trembling sides.
What had that ferment to do with her,
so secret, so alone, a separate creature?
Her small belly fattened, the breasts he had taught her were beau-
    tiful
swelled like melons, the nipples darkened. A turmoil
churned inside her, sharp and hard, a sack
of quarreling pullets, something all bone and beak.

Something of her, but alien. The first pain
rippled across her like a caress, so fleetingly
it fell. From her ankles a blush rose and branched
to all parts of her body. She panted, splashing
cold water onto her face from a stream. Crouched
in the shade of a bush she felt the waves begin.
She breathed with them. Once, under her feet,
the earth had billowed that way, rumbled, shifted,
then rent, dislodging the trees. Her nails bit the cheeks
of her palms. What was this uprooting, this quake?
Her limbs flew from her center, suddenly struck
in a black cataclysm, a flick that cleft
her two parts. She fell, fell into the wound.
It was this she had waited for, His transfixing hand!

Beth Bentley

245

Morning Song

Love set you going like a fat gold watch.
The midwife slapped your footsoles, and your bald cry
Took its place among the elements.

Our voices echo, magnifying your arrival. New statue.
In a drafty museum, your nakedness
Shadows our safety. We stand round blankly as walls.

I'm no more your mother
Than the cloud that distils a mirror to reflect its own slow
Effacement at the wind's hand.

All night your moth-breath
Flickers among the flat pink roses. I wake to listen:
A far sea moves in my ear.

One cry, and I stumble from bed, cow-heavy and floral
In my Victorian nightgown.
Your mouth opens clean as a cat's. The window square

Whitens and swallows its dull stars. And now you try
Your handful of notes;
The clear vows rise like balloons.

Sylvia Plath

Parting at Dawn

If there was a broken whispering by night
It was an image of the coward heart,
But the white dawn assures them how to part—
Stoics are born on the cold glitter of light,
And with the morning star lovers take flight.
Say, then, your parting; and most dry should you drain
Your lips of their wine, your eyes of the frantic rain,
Till these be as the barren cenobite.

And then? O dear Sir, stumbling down the street,
Continue, till you come to wars and wounds;
Beat the air, Madam, till your house-clock sounds;
And if no Lethe flows beneath your casement,
And when ten years have not brought full effacement,
Philosophy was wrong, and you may meet.

John Crowe Ransom

Dark Rosaleen

O my dark Rosaleen,
  Do not sigh, do not weep!
The priests are on the ocean green,
  They march along the deep.
There's wine from the royal Pope,
  Upon the ocean green;
And Spanish ale shall give you hope,
  My Dark Rosaleen!
  My own Rosaleen!

247

Shall glad your heart, shall give you hope,
Shall give you health, and help, and hope.
   My Dark Rosaleen!

Over hills, and thro' dales,
   Have I roam'd for your sake;
All yesterday I sail'd with sails
   On river and on lake.
The Erne, at its highest flood,
   I dash'd across unseen,
For there was lightning in my blood,
   My Dark Rosaleen!

   My own Rosaleen!
O, there was lightning in my blood,
Red lightning lighten'd thro' my blood.
   My Dark Rosaleen!

All day long, in unrest,
   To and fro, do I move.
The very soul within my breast
   Is wasted for you, love!
The heart in my bosom faints
   To think of you, my Queen,
My life of life, my saint of saints,
   My Dark Rosaleen!
   My own Rosaleen!
To hear your sweet and sad complaints,
My life, my love, my saint of saints,
   My Dark Rosaleen!

Woe and pain, pain and woe,
   Are my lot, night and noon,
To see your bright face clouded so,
   Like to the mournful moon.
But yet will I rear your throne
   Again in golden sheen;

'Tis you shall reign, shall reign alone,
   My Dark Rosaleen!
   My own Rosaleen!
'Tis you shall have the golden throne,
'Tis you shall reign, and reign alone,
   My Dark Rosaleen!

Over dews, over sands,
   Will I fly, for your weal:
Your holy delicate white hands
   Shall girdle me with steel.
At home, in your emerald bowers,
   From morning's dawn till e'en,
You'll pray for me, my flower of flowers,
   My Dark Rosaleen!
   My fond Rosaleen!
You'll think of me through daylight hours
My virgin flower, my flower of flowers,
   My Dark Rosaleen!

I could scale the blue air,
   I could plough the high hills,
Oh, I could kneel all night in prayer,
   To heal your many ills!
And one beamy smile from you
   Would float like light between
My toils and me, my own, my true,
   My Dark Rosaleen!
   My fond Rosaleen!
Would give me life and soul anew,
A second life, a soul anew,
   My Dark Rosaleen!

O, the Erne shall run red,
   With redundance of blood,
The earth shall rock beneath our tread,
   And flames wrap hill and wood,

And gun-peal and slogan-cry
　　Wake many a glen serene,
Ere you shall fade, ere you shall die,
　　My Dark Rosaleen!
　　My own Rosaleen!
The Judgement Hour must first be nigh,
Ere you can fade, ere you can die,
　　My Dark Rosaleen!

Anonymous
*Translated from the Gaelic
by James Clarence Mangan*

Sonnet to My Mother

Most near, most dear, most loved and most far,
Under the window where I often found her
Sitting as huge as Asia, seismic with laughter,
Gin and chicken helpless in her Irish hand,
Irresistible as Rabelais but most tender for
The lame dogs and hurt birds that surround her,—
She is a procession no one can follow after
But be like a little dog following a brass band.

She will not glance up at the bomber or condescend
To drop her gin and scuttle to a cellar,
But lean on the mahogany table like a mountain
Whom only faith can move, and so I send
O all my faith and all my love to tell her
That she will move from mourning into morning.

George Barker

Loves of the Puppets

Meeting when all the world was in the bud,
Drawn each to each by instinct's wooden face,
These lovers, heedful of the mystic blood,
Fell glassy-eyed into a hot embrace.

April, unready to be so intense,
Marked time while these outstripped the gentle weather,
Yielded their natures to insensate sense,
And flew apart the more they came together.

Where did they fly? Why, each through such a storm
As may be conjured in a globe of glass
Drove on the colder as the flesh grew warm,
In breathless haste to be at lust's impasse,

To cross the little bridge and sink to rest
In visions of the snow-occluded house
Where languishes, unfound by any quest,
The perfect, small, asphyxiated spouse.

That blizzard ended, and their eyes grew clear,
And there they lay exhausted yet unsated.
Why did their features run with tear on tear,
Until their looks were individuated?

One peace implies another, and they cried
For want of love as if their souls would crack,
Till in despair of being satisfied
They vowed at least to share each other's lack;

Then maladroitly they embraced once more,
And hollow rang to hollow with a sound
That tuned the brooks more sweetly than before
And made the birds explode for miles around.

Richard Wilbur

The Equilibrists

Full of her long white arms and milky skin
He had a thousand times remembered sin.
Alone in the press of people traveled he,
Minding her jacinth, and myrrh, and ivory.

Mouth he remembered: the quaint orifice
From which came heat that flamed upon the kiss,
Till cold words came down spiral from the head.
Grey doves from the officious tower illsped.

Body: it was a white field ready for love,
On her body's field, with the gaunt tower above,
The lilies grew, beseeching him to take,
If he would pluck and wear them, bruise and break.

Eyes talking: Never mind the cruel words,
Embrace my flowers, but not embrace the swords.
But what they said, the doves came straightway flying
And unsaid: Honor, Honor, they came crying.

Importunate her doves. Too pure, too wise,
Clambering on his shoulder, saying, Arise,
Leave me now, and never let us meet,
Eternal distance now command thy feet.

Predicament indeed, which thus discovers
Honor among thieves, Honor between lovers.
O such a little word is Honor, they feel!
But the grey word is between them cold as steel.

At length I saw these lovers fully were come
Into their torture of equilibrium;
Dreadfully had forsworn each other, and yet
They were bound each to each, and they did not forget.

And rigid as two painful stars, and twirled
About the clustered night their prison world,
They burned with fierce love always to come near,
But honor beat them back and kept them clear.

Ah, the strict lovers, they are ruined now!
I cried in anger. But with puddled brow
Devising for those gibbeted and brave
Came I descanting: Man, what would you have?

For spin your period out, and draw your breath,
A kinder saeculum begins with Death.
Would you ascend to Heaven and bodiless dwell?
Or take your bodies honorless to Hell?

In Heaven you have heard no marriage is,
No white flesh tinder to your lecheries,
Your male and female tissue sweetly shaped
Sublimed away, and furious blood escaped.

Great lovers lie in Hell, the stubborn ones
Infatuate of the flesh upon the bones;
Stuprate, they rend each other when they kiss,
The pieces kiss again, no end to this.

But still I watched them spinning, orbited nice.
Their flames were not more radiant than their ice.
I dug in the quiet earth and wrought the tomb
And made these lines to memorize their doom:—

EPITAPH

Equilibrists lie here; stranger, tread light;
Close, but untouching in each other's sight;
Mouldered the lips and ashy the tall skull.
Let them lie perilous and beautiful.

John Crowe Ransom

Elizabeth

An unaccustomed ripeness in the wood:
move but an inch and moldy splinters fall
in sawdust from the walls' aluminum-paint,
once loud and fresh, now aged to weathered wood.
Squalls of the seagull's exaggerated outcry
dim out in the fog. . . . *Pace, pace.* All day our words
were rusty fish-hooks—wormwood . . . Dear Heart's-Ease,
we rest from all discussion, drinking, smoking,
pills for high blood, three pairs of glasses—soaking
in the sweat of our hard-earned supremacy,
offering a child our leathery love. We're fifty,
and free! Young, tottering on the dizzying brink
of discretion once, you wanted nothing,
but to be old, do nothing, type and think.

Robert Lowell

9

*"For still I am as always my heart's
hungering slave . . ."*

"Are you the new person drawn toward me?"

Are you the new person drawn toward me?
To begin with, take warning, I am surely far different from what
    you suppose;
Do you suppose you will find in me your ideal?
Do you think it so easy to have me become your lover?
Do you think the friendship of me would be unalloy'd satisfaction?
Do you think I am trusty and faithful?
Do you see no further than this facade, this smooth and tolerant
    manner of me?
Do you suppose yourself advancing on real ground toward a real
    heroic man?
Have you no thought, O dreamer, that it may be all maya, illusion?

Walt Whitman

Touch

You are already
asleep. I lower
myself in next to
you, my skin slightly
numb with the restraint
of habits, the patina of
self, the black frost
of outsideness, so that even
unclothed it is

256

a resilient chilly
hardness, a superficially
malleable, dead
rubbery texture.

You are a mound
of bedclothes, where the cat
in sleep braces
its paws against your
calf through the blankets,
and kneads each paw in turn.

Meanwhile and slowly
I feel a is it
my own warmth surfacing or
the ferment of your whole
body that in darkness beneath
the cover is stealing
bit by bit to break
down that chill.

           You turn and
hold me tightly, do
you know who
I am or am I
your mother or
the nearest human being to
hold on to in a
dreamed pogrom.

What I, now loosened,
sink into is an old
big place, it is
there already, for
you are already
there, and the cat
got there before you, yet

it is hard to locate.
What is more, the place is
not found but seeps
from our touch in
continuous creation, dark
enclosing cocoon round
ourselves alone, dark
wide realm where we
walk with everyone.

Thom Gunn

For the Book of Love

I may be dead to-morrow, uncaressed.
   My lips have never touched a woman's, none
   Has given me in a look her soul, not one
Has ever held me swooning at her breast.

I have but suffered, for all nature, trees
   Whipped by the winds, wan flowers, the ashen sky,
   Suffered with all my nerves, minutely, I
Have suffered for my soul's impurities.

And I have spat on love, and, mad with pride,
   Slaughtered my flesh, and life's revenge I brave,
   And, while the whole world else was Instinct's slave,
With bitter laughter Instinct I defied.

In drawing-rooms, the theater, the church,
   Before cold men, the greatest, most refined,
   And women with eyes jealous, proud, or kind,
Whose tender souls no lust would seem to smirch,

I thought: This is the end for which they work.
   Beasts coupling with the groaning beasts they capture.
   And all this dirt for just three minutes' rapture!
Men, be correct! And women, purr and smirk!

Jules Laforgue
*Translated from the French
by Jethro Bithell*

John Anderson My Jo

John Anderson my jo, John,
   When we were first acquent,
Your locks were like the raven,
   Your bonie brow was brent;
But now your brow is beld, John,
   Your locks are like the snaw,
But blessings on your frosty pow,
   John Anderson my jo!

John Anderson my jo, John,
   We clamb the hill thegither,
And monie a cantie day, John,
   We've had wi' ane anither;
Now we maun totter down, John,
   And hand in hand we'll go,
And sleep thegither at the foot,
   John Anderson my jo!

Robert Burns

How Can I Keep My Maidenhead

How can I keep my maidenhead,
   My maidenhead, my maidenhead;
How can I keep my maidenhead,
   Among sae mony men, O.

The Captain bad a guinea for't,
   A guinea for't, a guinea for't;
The Captain bad a guinea for't,
   The Colonel he bad ten, O.

But I'll do as my minnie did,
   My minnie did, my minnie did;
But I'll do as my minnie did,
   For siller I'll hae nane, O.

I'll gie it to a bonie lad,
   A bonie lad, a bonie lad;
I'll gie it to a bonie lad,
   For just as gude again, O.

An auld moulie maidenhead,
   A maidenhead, a maidenhead;
An auld moulie maidenhead,
   The weary wark I ken, O.

The stretchin' o't, the strivin' o't,
   The borin' o't, the rivin' o't,
And ay the double drivin' o't,
   The farther ye gang ben, O.

Robert Burns

Astrophel and Stella I: *"Loving in truth, and fain in verse my love to show"*

Loving in truth, and fain in verse my love to show,
That She, dear She, might take some pleasure of my pain,
Pleasure might cause her read, reading might make her know,
Knowledge might pity win, and pity grace obtain,
I sought fit words to paint the blackest face of woe;
Studying inventions fine, her wits to entertain,
Oft turning others' leaves, to see if thence would flow
Some fresh and fruitful showers upon my sun-burn'd brain.
But words came halting out, wanting Invention's stay;
Invention, Nature's child, fled stepdame Study's blows;
And others' feet still seem'd but strangers in my way.
Thus, great with child to speak, and helpless in my throes,
Biting my truant pen, beating myself for spite,
'Fool,' said my Muse to me, 'look in thy heart and write.'

Sir Philip Sidney

The Goose Fish

On the long shore, lit by the moon
To show them properly alone,
Two lovers suddenly embraced
So that their shadows were as one.
The ordinary night was graced
For them by the swift tide of blood
That silently they took at flood,
And for a little time they prized
    Themselves emparadised.

261

Then, as if shaken by stage-fright
Beneath the hard moon's bony light,
They stood together on the sand
Embarrassed in each other's sight
But still conspiring hand in hand,
Until they saw, there underfoot,
As though the world had found them out,
The goose fish turning up, though dead,
        His hugely grinning head.

There in the china light he lay,
Most ancient and corrupt and grey.
They hesitated at his smile,
Wondering what it seemed to say
To lovers who a little while
Before had thought to understand,
By violence upon the sand,
The only way that could be known
        To make a world their own.

It was a wide and moony grin
Together peaceful and obscene;
They knew not what he would express,
So finished a comedian
He might mean failure or success,
But took it for an emblem of
Their sudden, new and guilty love
To be observed by, when they kissed,
        That rigid optimist.

So he became their patriarch,
Dreadfully mild in the half-dark.
His throat that the sand seemed to choke,
His picket teeth, these left their mark
But never did explain the joke

That so amused him, lying there
While the moon went down to disappear
Along the still and tilted track
        That bears the zodiac.

Howard Nemerov

Dreamed-Up for Winter

This winter in a rosy railroad car
        With blue upholstery
We shall be snug. Nestsful of kisses are
        Waiting for us in every padded cranny.

You with your eyes shut tight so you won't see
        Evening shadows—
Demons, black wolves and cross monstrosities
        Glare through the windows.

Then on your cheek a scratch or something lighter
A tiny kiss which runs like a panicked spider
        Downward somewhere out of touch . . .

And you will tell me "Look for it!" with a gesture.
And we will take our time finding this creature
        —Who moves about so much . . .

Arthur Rimbaud
*Translated from the French
by William Mead*

Lost Desire

Love brought by night a vision to my bed,
One that still wore the vesture of a child
But eighteen years of age—who sweetly smiled
Till of the lovely form false hopes were bred
    And keen embraces wild.
Ah! for the lost desire that haunts me yet,
Till mine eyes fail in sleep that finds no more
That fleeting ghost! Oh, lovelorn heart, give o'er—
Cease thy vain dreams of beauty's warmth—forget
    The face thou longest for!

Meleager
Translated from the Greek
by William M. Hardinge

"Will you perhaps consent to be"

"méntre il vento, come fa, si tace"

Will you perhaps consent to be
Now that a little while is still
(Ruth of sweet wind) now that a little while
My mind's continuing and unreleasing wind
Touches this single of your flowers, this one only,
Will you perhaps consent to be
My many-branched, small and dearest tree?

My mind's continuing and unreleasing wind
—The wind which is wild and restless, tired and asleep,
The wind which is tired, wild and still continuing,
The wind which is chill, and warm, wet, soft, in every influence,
Lusts for Paris, Crete and Pergamus,

264

Is suddenly off for Paris and Chicago,
Judaea, San Francisco, the Midi
—May I perhaps return to you
Wet with an Attic dust and chill from Norway
My dear, so-many-branched smallest tree?

Would you perhaps consent to be
The very rack and crucifix of winter, winter's wild
Knife-edged, continuing and unreleasing,
Intent and stripping, ice-caressing wind?
My dear, most dear, so-many-branched tree
My mind's continuing and unreleasing wind
Touches this single of your flowers, faith in me,
Wide as the—sky!—accepting as the (air)!
—Consent, consent, consent to be
My many-branched, small and dearest tree.

Delmore Schwartz

A *Drifting*

I had a sister once, an island sister
Younger than I, and silent, slow in school.
In the midst of our games she would stand with foundling eyes,
Hands finding a hem, lips clenched in a smile.

That day was cloudless: hilltopped, my brothers and I,
Grouped by the wind, tossed rocks at winter, waited
For smoke in the sky. My sister, beckoned by stones
And turtles, her skirts tucked high, waded
The matron shore. Her legs gone,
Bobbed on the careless waters like a floated ball,
She seemed intent
On some lost game the sea composed.

Birds did not hear the beckon that she sent.
The small ships hardly moved at all.

I think of her sometimes, beyond our sight,
Tagged by the sun where the dark fish play:
In the cold, a fragile island of delight
Beyond our voice—
        We are not brothers of the sea.

Robert Hutchinson

Morning Worship

I wake and hear it raining.
Were I dead, what would I give
Lazily to lie here,
Like this, and live?

Or better yet: birdsong,
Brightening and spreading—
How far would I come then
To be at the world's wedding?

Now that I lie, though,
Listening, living,
(Oh, but not forever,
Oh, end arriving)

How shall I praise them:
All the sweet beings
Eternally that outlive
Me and my dying?

Mountains, I mean; wind, water, air;
Grass, and huge trees; clouds, flowers,
And thunder, and night.

Turtles, I mean, and toads; hawks, herons, owls;
Graveyards, and towns, and trout; roads, gardens,
Red berries, and deer.

Lightning, I mean, and eagles; fences; snow;
Sunrise, and ferns; waterfalls, serpents,
Green islands, and sleep.

Horses, I mean; butterflies, whales;
Mosses, and stars; and gravelly
Rivers, and fruit.

Oceans, I mean; black valleys; corn;
Brambles, and cliffs; rock, dirt, dust, ice;
And warnings of flood.

How shall I name them?
And in what order?
Each would be first.
Omission is murder.

Maidens, I mean, and apples; needles; leaves;
Worms, and planets, and clover; whirlwinds; dew;
Bulls; geese—

Stop. Lie still.
You will never be done.
Leave them all there,
Old lover. Live on.

Mark Van Doren

The Phantom Horsewoman

I

Queer are the ways of a man I know:
      He comes and stands
      In a careworn craze,
      And looks at the sands
      And the seaward haze
      With moveless hands
      And face and gaze,
      Then turns to go . . .
And what does he see when he gazes so?

II

They say he sees as an instant thing
      More clear than to-day,
      A sweet soft scene
      That once was in play
      By that briny green;
      Yes, notes alway
      Warm, real, and keen,
      What his back years bring—
A phantom of his own figuring.

III

Of this vision of his they might say more:
      Not only there
      Does he see this sight,
      But everywhere

In his brain—day, night,
As if on the air
It were drawn rose bright—
Yea, far from that shore
Does he carry this vision of heretofore:

IV

A ghost-girl-rider. And though, toil-tried,
　　He withers daily,
　　Time touches her not,
　　But she still rides gaily
　　In his rapt thought
　　On that shagged and shaly
　　Atlantic spot,
　　And as when first eyed
Draws rein and sings to the swing of the tide.

Thomas Hardy

Tantalos

Mouth to mouth joined we lie, her naked breasts
Curved to my fingers, my fury grazing deep
On the silver plain of her throat,
　　　　　　　and then: no more.
She denies me her bed. Half of her body to Love
She has given, half to Prudence:
　　　　　　I die between.

Paulus Silentarius
*Translated from the Latin
by Dudley Fitts*

Poet's Wish

When I have been dead for several years
And cabs in the fog still collide
As they do today (things not having changed)
May I be a cool hand upon some forehead!
On the forehead of someone humming in a carriage
Along Brompton Road, Marylebone or Holborn,
Who, thinking of literature,
Looks out through the yellow fog at the great black monuments.
Yes, may I be the dark, gentle thought
One bears secretly in the noise of cities,
A moment's repose in the wind that drives us on,
Lost children in a fair of vanities;
And may my humble beginning in eternity be honored
On All Saint's Day with a simple ornament, a little moss.

Valery Larbaud
*Translated from the French
by William Jay Smith*

"Elysium is as far as to"

Elysium is as far as to
The very nearest Room
If in that Room a Friend await
Felicity or Doom—

What fortitude the Soul contains,
That it can so endure
The accent of a coming Foot—
The opening of a Door—

                              Emily Dickinson

A Face

If one could have that little head of hers
   Painted upon a background of pale gold,
Such as the Tuscan's early art prefers!
   No shade encroaching on the matchless mould
Of those two lips, which should be opening soft
   In the pure profile; not as when she laughs,
For that spoils all: but rather as if aloft
   Yon hyacinth, she loves so, leaned its staff's
Burthen of honey-coloured buds to kiss
And capture 'twixt the lips apart for this.
Then her lithe neck, three fingers might surround,
How it should waver on the pale gold ground
Up to the fruit-shaped, perfect chin it lifts!
I know, Correggio loves to mass, in rifts
Of heaven, his angel faces, orb on orb
Breaking its outline, burning shades absorb:
But these are only massed there, I should think,
   Waiting to see some wonder momently
   Grow out, stand full, fade slow against the sky
   (That's the pale ground you'd see this sweet face by),
   All heaven, meanwhile, condensed into one eye
Which fears to lose the wonder, should it wink.

Robert Browning

The Haunter

He does not think that I haunt here nightly:
   How shall I let him know
That whither his fancy sets him wandering
   I, too, alertly go?—

Hover and hover a few feet from him
    Just as I used to do,
But cannot answer the words he lifts me—
    Only listen thereto!

When I could answer he did not say them:
    When I could let him know
How I would like to join in his journeys
    Seldom he wished to go.
Now that he goes and wants me with him
    More than he used to do,
Never he sees my faithful phantom
    Though he speaks thereto.

Yes, I companion him to places
    Only dreamers know,
Where the shy hares print long paces,
    Where the night rooks go;
Into old aisles where the past is all to him,
    Close as his shade can do,
Always lacking the power to call to him,
    Near as I reach thereto!

What a good haunter I am, O tell him!
    Quickly make him know
If he but sigh since my loss befell him
    Straight to his side I go.
Tell him a faithful one is doing
    All that love can do
Still that his path may be worth pursuing,
    And to bring peace thereto.

Thomas Hardy

At Night

In the dust are my father's beautiful hands,
In the dust are my mother's eyes.
Here by the shore of the ocean standing,
Watching: still I do not understand.

Love flows over me, around me,
Here at night by the sea, by the sovereign sea.

Gone is that bone-hoard of strength;
Gone her gentle motion laughing, walking.

Is it not strange that disease and death
Should rest, by the undulant sea?

And I stare, rich with gifts, alone,

Feeling from the sea those terrene presences,
My father's hands, my mother's eyes.

Richard Eberhart

Nudes

(Adieus. Absence. Return.)

The moon was born grey, and Beethoven was weeping
Beneath her white hands, within her piano . . .
In the unlit living room, she was, as she played,
Dark with moonlight and three times as lovely.

The flowers of our two hearts were bleeding to death
And perhaps we wept without either seeing the tears . . .
Each note set afire one of the wounds of love . . .
The sweet piano endeavored to understand us.

From the balcony, open to the misty starlight,
A sad wind came, from invisible worlds . . .
And she, she asked me about things unknowable
And I answered her with unattainable things.

Juan Ramón Jiménez

The Little Brother

God! how they plague his life, the three damned sisters,
Throwing stones at him out of the cherry trees,
Pulling his hair, smudging his exercises,
Whispering. How passionately he sees
His spilt minnows flounder in the grass.

There will be sisters subtler far than these,
Baleful and dark, with slender, cared-for hands,
Who will not smirk and babble in the trees,
But feed him with sweet words and provocations,
And in his sleep practise their sorceries,
Appearing in the form of ragged clouds
And at the corners of malignant seas.

As with his wounded life he goes alone
To the world's end, where even tears freeze,
He will in bitter memory and remorse
Hear the lost sisters innocently tease.

James Reeves

"All is well with the child"

I saw you arise from your bed, I saw your door open
Into a room flowering and falling with flame,
Into that room you came.
I feared for you, I followed, I called your name:

And you walked unharmed through the fire three times in flame,
You plunged and scorched to the soul returned, renewed, un-
    harmed,
And the flames thinned to ashes, fell in a waiting urn.

Pallid with dying light I saw the day return.

No mind could penetrate, no eye discern
In what perpetual lives and deaths you breathed and drew
Strength for another life, another death.
That all was well with you the awakening sunlight knew.

Then without anguish, indifferent, calm, and reconciled
I heard the voice of my heart: "All is well with the child,
And lilacs sprang into bloom, it was spring, the air was mild,
And again the voice said: "All is well with the child."

Marya Zaturenska

Sonnet IV: *"My love, I have betrayed you seventy times"*

My love, I have betrayed you seventy times
In this brief period since our stars were met:
Against your ghost announced unnumbered crimes,
And many times its image overset;
Forgot you, worshipped others, flung a flower
To meaner beauty, proved an infidel;
Showing my heart not loyal beyond an hour,
Betraying Paradise, and invoking Hell.
Alas! what chain of thought can thinking bind?
It is in thought alone that I have faltered,
It is my fugitive and quicksilver mind,
By every chance and change too lightly altered.
Can I absolve, from this all-staining sin,
The angelic love who sits, ashamed, within?

Conrad Aiken

The Double Shame

You must live through the time when everything hurts
When the space of the ripe, loaded afternoon
Expands to a landscape of white heat frozen
And trees are weighed down with hearts of stone
And green stares back where you stare alone,
And the walking eyes throw flinty comments
And the words which carry most knives are the blind
Phrases searching to be kind.

277

Solid and usual objects are ghosts
The furniture carries cargoes of memory,
The staircase has corners which remember
As fire blows red in gusty embers,
And each empty dress cuts out an image
In fur and evening and summer and gold
Of her who was different in each.

Pull down the blind and lie on the bed
And clasp the hour in the glass of one room
Against your mouth like a crystal doom.
Take up the book and look at the letters
Hieroglyphs on sand and as meaningless—
Here birds crossed once and cries were uttered
In a mist where sight and sound are blurred.

For the story of those who made mistakes
Of one whose happiness pierced like a star
Eludes and evades between sentences
And the letters break into eyes which read
What the blood is now writing in your head,
As though the characters sought for some clue
To their being so perfectly living and dead
In your story, worse than theirs, but true.

Set in the mind of their poet, they compare
Their tragic bliss with your trivial despair
And they have fingers which accuse
You of the double way of shame.
At first you did not love enough
And afterwards you loved too much
And you lacked the confidence to choose
And you have only yourself to blame.

Stephen Spender

The Amorous Worms' Meat

When my heart was the amorous worms' meat
And did in amorous consumption rave,
I sought the scattered footsteps of a sweet
Wild animal through wood and hill and cave;
And I dared in my singing to complain
Of Love, of her, who seemed to scorn my pain.
But my genius and rhymes were much too weak
In that new age for thoughts so young and sick.
That fire is dead, in a small marble press.
Ah, if with time it had increased in rage
As in the past, until my oldest age,
Armed with my rhymes that now I leave alone,
My gray-haired style would have broken a stone
With words, and made it weep from tenderness.

Francesco Petrarca
Translated from the Italian
by Anna Maria Armi

Sonnet LXXXVII: "Farewell! thou art too dear for my possessing"

Farewell! thou art too dear for my possessing,
And like enough thou know'st thy estimate:
The charter of thy worth gives thee releasing;
My bonds in thee are all determinate.
For how do I hold thee but by thy granting?
And for that riches where is my deserving?
The cause of this fair gift in me is wanting,

And so my patent back again is swerving.
Thyself thou gavest, thy own worth then not knowing,
Or me, to whom thou gavest it, else mistaking;
So thy great gift, upon misprision growing,
Comes home again, on better judgement making.
Thus have I had thee, as a dream doth flatter,
In sleep a king, but waking no such matter.

William Shakespeare

" 'Twas a long Parting—but the time"

'Twas a long Parting—but the time
For Interview—had come—
Before the Judgment Seat of God—
The last—and second time

These Fleshless Lovers met—
A Heaven in a Gaze—
A Heaven of Heavens—the Privilege
Of one another's Eyes—

No Lifetime set—on Them—
Appareled as the new
Unborn—except They had beheld—
Born infiniter—now—

Was Bridal—e'er like This?
A Paradise—the Host—
And Cherubim—and Seraphim—
The unobtrusive Guest—

Emily Dickinson

10

"Straw-in-the-fire love,
It's no morality play we're in . . ."

"To Speak of My Influences"

To speak of my influences:
Above all, your eyes,
And next, that jar of the bell
When I think it is you who call.
Since half the time it is not,
I have fevers to quell.
To speak as well
Of the rain in the night
We suddenly heard lying there,
That satin'd stress of a crazy wine
Silverly beating down.
That music, too, you played—
Or was it your élan,
Dense and rich? A sea-clashed mist
Warred with the wracked pulse
That danced my blood to flame
Plagued by certain notes
Of irritable brilliance and flutes
Velvet-mouthed. Ah, monotone
Of phrases faded into dissolution!
Dazed, credulous, I lived
Unbalanced by such powers
As ruled me like that speech you played
And rain's metallic waterfalls.
They ruled me, yes. Eyes kissed by eyes
And ears stunned by the delicacy
Of that fire-in-the-straw art
Wished no more than to be
Set once more alight.

To speak of my influences:
By force of fate, you said,
Who came with masks, imported more
When the suave cords were twanged,
Increased the speed at which it wound
Its flaunting silk of sound.
O heresy! All changes
Save this art at which we play,
The instant, drenched in rain,
We imitated once again
But have we the cunning to
Keep enthrallment vined?

Straw-in-the-fire love,
It's no morality play we're in,
Nor can we trick time
Nor end where we began.
Let us end as we will
While I make apostrophes
That will not more excel
Than your eyes, our dance,
And we'll love on by chance.

Jean Garrigue

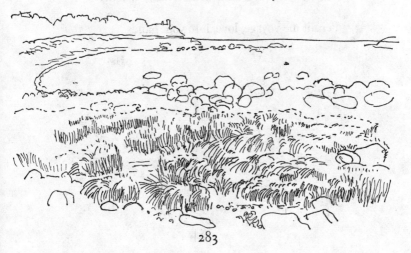

283

Voyages III: *"Infinite consanguinity it bears"*

Infinite consanguinity it bears—
This tendered theme of you that light
Retrieves from sea plains where the sky
Resigns a breast that every wave enthrones;
While ribboned water lanes I wind
Are laved and scattered with no stroke
Wide from your side, whereto this hour
The sea lifts, also, reliquary hands.

And so, admitted through black swollen gates
That must arrest all distance otherwise,—
Past whirling pillars and lithe pediments,
Light wrestling there incessantly with light,
Star kissing star through wave on wave unto
Your body rocking!

              and where death, if shed,
Presumes no carnage, but this single change,—
Upon the steep floor flung from dawn to dawn
The silken skilled transmemberment of song;

Permit me voyage, love, into your hands . . .

                           Hart Crane

"O where is the dwelling"

O where is the dwelling I love the most,
And what but the one poor place can please,
Where the penny I lost and the faith I lost
Lie buried beneath enchanted trees?

O there is the dwelling I love the most,
And thither for ever my feet are bound,
Where the youth I lost and the love I lost
Lie buried, lie buried in holy ground!

Ruth Pitter

"Since there's no help, come let us kiss and part"

Since there 's no help, come let us kiss and part—
Nay, I have done: you get no more of me;
And I am glad, yea, glad with all my heart,
That thus so cleanly I myself can free.
Shake hands for ever, cancel all our vows,
And when we meet at any time again,
Be it not seen in either of our brows
That we one jot of former love retain.
Now at the last gasp of love's latest breath,
When, his pulse failing, Passion speechless lies,
When Faith is kneeling by his bed of death,
And Innocence is closing up his eyes,—
　Now, if thou wouldst, when all have given him over,
　From death to life thou might'st him yet recover!

Michael Drayton

Two Loves

That her serene influence should spread
An afternoon of soft autumnal light
Is to my heart not unaccountable
For she was young, and is not dead.
And still her cheek is red and white.

But that this stealthy still insistent power
Pervades my mind and will not slumber me
Is delicate woe and glory hard to bear;
Her life lives in a ghost-wrought hour,
From whose chill spirit I am not free.

The one was willow to an ardent touch
And she was mood that had a right to die.
But she, the other, the passion of my mind
Long-living still, does overmuch
Come from the dead, and from the sky.

                                        Richard Eberhart

"when the proficient poison of sure sleep"

when the proficient poison of sure sleep
bereaves us of our slow tranquilities

and He without Whose favour nothing is
(being of men called Love) upward doth leap
from the mute hugeness of depriving deep,

with thunder of those hungering wings of His,

286

into the lucent and large signories
—i shall not smile beloved; i shall not weep:

when from the less-than-whiteness of thy face
(whose eyes inherit vacancy) will time
extract his inconsiderable doom,
when these thy lips beautifully embrace
nothing
        and when thy bashful hands assume

silence beyond the mystery of rhyme

                        E. E. Cummings

In Love for Long

I've been in love for long
With what I cannot tell
And will contrive a song
For the intangible
That has no mould or shape,
From which there's no escape.

It is not even a name,
Yet is all constancy;
Tried or untried, the same,
It cannot part from me;
A breath, yet as still
As the established hill.

It is not any thing,
And yet all being is;
Being, being, being,
Its burden and its bliss.
How can I ever prove
What it is I love?

287

This happy happy love
Is sieged with crying sorrows,
Crushed beneath and above
Between to-days and morrows;
A little paradise
Held in the world's vice.

And there it is content
And careless as a child,
And in imprisonment
Flourishes sweet and wild;
In wrong, beyond wrong,
All the world's day long.

This love a moment known
For what I do not know
And in a moment gone
Is like the happy doe
That keeps its perfect laws
Between the tiger's paws
And vindicates its cause.

Edwin Muir

"*somewhere i have never travelled, gladly beyond*"

somewhere i have never travelled, gladly beyond
any experience, your eyes have their silence:
in your most frail gesture are things which enclose me
or which i cannot touch because they are too near

your slightest look easily will unclose me
though i have closed myself as fingers,
you open always petal by petal myself as Spring opens
(touching skilfully, mysteriously) her first rose

or if your wish be to close me, i and
my life will shut very beautifully, suddenly,
as when the heart of this flower imagines
the snow carefully everywhere descending;

nothing which we are to perceive in this world equals
the power of your intense fragility: whose texture
compels me with the colour of its countries,
rendering death and forever with each breathing

(i do not know what it is about you that closes
and opens; only something in me understands
the voice of your eyes is deeper than all roses)
nobody, not even the rain, has such small hands

E. E. Cummings

Peter Quince at the Clavier

I

Just as my fingers on these keys
Make music, so the selfsame sounds
On my spirit make a music, too.

Music is feeling, then, not sound;
And thus it is that what I feel,
Here in this room, desiring you,

Thinking of your blue-shadowed silk,
Is music. It is like the strain
Waked in the elders by Susanna.

Of a green evening, clear and warm,
She bathed in her still garden, while
The red-eyed elders watching, felt

The basses of their beings throb
In witching chords, and their thin blood
Pulse pizzicati of Hosanna.

II

In the green water, clear and warm,
Susanna lay.
She searched
The touch of springs,
And found
Concealed imaginings.
She sighed
For so much melody.

Upon the bank, she stood
In the cool
Of spent emotions.
She felt, among the leaves,
The dew
Of old devotions.

She walked upon the grass,
Still quavering.
The winds were like her maids,
On timid feet,
Fetching her woven scarves,
Yet wavering.

A breath upon her hand
Muted the night.
She turned—
A cymbal crashed,
And roaring horns.

III

Soon, with a noise like tambourines,
Came her attendant Byzantines.

They wondered why Susanna cried
Against the elders by her side;
And as they whispered, the refrain
Was like a willow swept by rain.

Anon, their lamps' uplifted flame
Revealed Susanna and her shame.

And then, the simpering Byzantines
Fled, with a noise like tambourines.

IV

Beauty is momentary in the mind—
The fitful tracing of a portal;
But in the flesh it is immortal.
The body dies; the body's beauty lives.
So evenings die, in their green going,
A wave, interminably flowing.
So gardens die, their meek breath scenting
The cowl of winter, done repenting.
So maidens die, to the auroral
Celebration of a maiden's choral.
Susanna's music touched the bawdy strings
Of those white elders; but, escaping,
Left only Death's ironic scraping.
Now, in its immortality, it plays
On the clear viol of her memory,
And makes a constant sacrament of praise.

Wallace Stevens

The Chosen

"A woman for whom great gods might strive!"
    I said, and kissed her there:
And then I thought of the other five,
    And of how charms outwear.

I thought of the first with her eating eyes,
And I thought of the second with hers, green-gray,
And I thought of the third, experienced, wise,
And I thought of the fourth who sang all day.

And I thought of the fifth, whom I'd called a jade.
    And I thought of them all, tear-fraught;
And that each had shown her a passable maid,
    Yet not of the favour sought.

So I traced these words on the bark of a beech,
Just at the falling of the mast:
"After scanning five; yes, each and each,
I've found the woman desired—at last!"

"—I feel a strange benumbing spell,
    As one ill-wished!" said she.
And soon it seemed that something fell
    Was starving her love for me.

"I feel some curse. O, *five* were there?"
And wanly she swerved, and went away.
I followed sick: night numbed the air,
And dark the mournful moorland lay.

I cried: "O darling, turn your head!"
    But never her face I viewed;
"O turn, O turn!" again I said,
    And miserably pursued.

At length I came to a Christ-cross stone
Which she had passed without discern;
And I knelt upon the leaves there strown,
And prayed aloud that she might turn.

I rose, and looked; and turn she did;
    I cried, "My heart revives!"
"Look more," she said. I looked as bid;
    Her face was all the five's.

All the five women, clear come back,
I saw in her—with her made one,
The while she drooped upon the track,
And her frail term seemed well-nigh run.

She'd half forgot me in her change;
    "Who are you? Won't you say
Who you may be, you man so strange,
    Following since yesterday?"

I took the composite form she was,
And carried her to an arbour small,
Not passion-moved, but even because
In one I could atone to all.

And there she lies, and there I tend,
    Till my life's threads unwind,
A various womanhood in blend—
    Not one, but all combined.

Thomas Hardy

A *Farewell to False Love*

Farewell, false love, the oracle of lies,
A mortal foe and enemy to rest,
An envious boy, from whom all cares arise,
A bastard vile, a beast with rage possessed,
A way of error, a temple full of treason,
In all effects contrary unto reason.

A poisoned serpent covered all with flowers,
Mother of sighs, and murderer of repose,
A sea of sorrows whence are drawn such showers
As moisture lend to every grief that grows;
A school of guile, a net of deep deceit,
A gilded hook that holds a poisoned bait.

A fortress foiled, which reason did defend,
A siren song, a fever of the mind,
A maze wherein affection finds no end,
A raging cloud that runs before the wind,
A substance like the shadow of the sun,
A goal of grief for which the wisest run.

A quenchless fire, a nurse of trembling fear,
A path that leads to peril and mishap,
A true retreat of sorrow and despair,
An idle boy that sleeps in pleasure's lap,
A deep mistrust of that which certain seems,
A hope of that which reason doubtful deems.

Sith then thy trains my younger years betrayed,
And for my faith ingratitude I find;
And sith repentance hath my wrongs bewrayed,
Whose course was ever contrary to kind:
False love, desire, and beauty frail, adieu!
Dead is the root whence all these fancies grew.

Sir Walter Raleigh

Villanelle

It is the pain, it is the pain, endures.
Your chemic beauty burned my muscles through.
Poise of my hands reminded me of yours.

What later purge from this deep toxin cures?
What kindness now could the old salve renew?
It is the pain, it is the pain, endures.

The infection slept (custom or change inures)
And when pain's secondary phase was due
Poise of my hands reminded me of yours.

How safe I felt, whom memory assures,
Rich that your grace safely by heart I knew.
It is the pain, it is the pain, endures.

My stare drank deep beauty that still allures.
My heart pumps yet the poison draught of you.
Poise of my hands reminded me of yours.

You are still kind whom the same shape immures.
Kind and beyond adieu. We miss our cue.
It is the pain, it is the pain, endures.
Poise of my hands reminded me of yours.

William Empson

Splendidis longum valedico nugis

Leave me, O love which reachest but to dust,
And thou, my mind, aspire to higher things.
Grow rich in that which never taketh rust:
Whatever fades but fading pleasure brings.
Draw in thy beams, and humble all thy might
To that sweet yoke where lasting freedoms be;
Which breaks the clouds and opens forth the light
That doth both shine and give us sight to see.
O take fast hold; let that light be thy guide
In this small course which birth draws out to death,
And think how evil becometh him to slide
Who seeketh heaven and comes of heavenly breath.
Then farewell, world! thy uttermost I see:
Eternal Love, maintain thy life in me.

Sir Philip Sidney

Apology for Understatement

Forgive me that I pitch your praise too low.
Such reticence my reverence demands,
For silence falls with laying on of hands.

Forgive me that my words come thin and slow.
This could not be a time for eloquence,
For silence falls with healing of the sense.

We only utter what we lightly know.
And it is rather that my love knows me.
It is that your perfection set me free.

296

Verse is dressed up that has nowhere to go.
You took away my glibness with my fear.
Forgive me that I stand in silence here.

It is not words could pay you what I owe.

John Wain

A *Fragment of Petronius Translated*

Foeda est in coitu et brevis voluptas

Doing a filthy pleasure is, and short;
And done, we straight repent us of the sport.
Let us not then rush blindly on unto it,
Like lustful beasts, that only know to do it;
For lust will languish, and that heat decay.
But thus, thus, keeping endless holiday,
Let us together closely lie, and kiss;
There is no labour nor no shame in this.
This hath pleased, doth please, and long will please; never
Can this decay, but is beginning ever.

Ben Jonson

Trilce XV: *"In that corner,* *where we slept together"*

In that corner, where we slept together
so many nights, I've sat down now
to take a walk. The bedstead of the dead lovers
has been taken away, or what could have happened.

You came early for other things,
but you've gone now. This is the corner
where I read one night, by your side,
between your tender breasts,
a story by Daudet. It is the corner
we loved. Don't confuse it with any other.

I've started to think about those days
of summer gone, with you entering and leaving,
little and fed up, pale through the rooms.

On this rainy night,
already far from both of us, all at once I jump . . .
two doors in the wind, back, and forth,
shadow   to   shadow.

César Vallejo
*Translated from the Spanish
by James Wright*

The Fitting

The fitter said, "Madame, vous avez maigri."
And pinched together a handful of skirt at my hip.
"Tant mieux," I said, and looked away slowly, and took my
    under-lip
Softly between my teeth.

        Rip-rip!
Out came the seam, and was pinned together in another place.
She knelt before me, a hardworking woman with a familiar and
    unknown face,
Dressed in linty black, very tight in the arm's-eye and smelling of
    sweat.
She rose, lifting my arm, and set her cold shears against me, snip-
    snip;

298

Her knuckles gouged my breast. My drooped eyes lifted to my
   guarded eyes in the glass, and glanced away as from someone
   they had never met.

"Ah, que madame a maigri!" cried the vendeuse, coming in with
   dresses over her arm.
"C'est la chaleur," I said, looking out into the sunny tops of the
   horse-chestnuts—and indeed it was very warm.

I stood for a long time so, looking out into the afternoon, thinking
   of the evening and you. . . .
While they murmured busily in the distance, turning me, touch-
   ing my secret body, doing what they were paid to do.

                                        Edna St. Vincent Millay

The Falcon Woman

It is hard to be a man
Whose word is his bond
In love with such a woman,

When he builds on a promise
She lightly let fall
In carelessness of spirit.

The more sternly he asks her
To stand by that promise
The faster she flies.

But is it less hard
To be born such a woman
With wings like a falcon
And in carelessness of spirit
To love such a man?

                                        Robert Graves

Sonnet V:
"IMPRIMIS: I forgot all day your face"

IMPRIMIS: I forgot all day your face,
Eyes, eyebrows, gentle mouth, and cheek, all faded;
Nor could I, in the mind's dark forest, trace
The haunted path whereby that dream evaded.
Secundus: I forgot all night your laughter,
In vain evoked it by strong charms of thought:
Gone, like a cry that leaves no image after,
Phoenix of sound which no hand ever caught.
Tertius: my wanton mind and heart, together,
Forgetting you, you absent, have delighted
For no more cause than bright or stormy weather,
Singing for joy; in truth, I am benighted.
Yet, when I home once more from breach of faith,
Love there awaits me with a joy like death.

Conrad Aiken

The Microcosm

Man of himself's a little world, but join'd
With woman, woman for that end design'd,
(Hear cruel fair one whilst I this rehearse!)
He makes up then a complete universe.
    Man, like this sublunary world, is born
The sport of two cross planets, love, and scorn:
Woman the other world resembles well,
In whose looks Heav'n is, in whose breast Hell.

Giovanni Battista Guarini
*Translated from the Italian
by Sir Edward Sherburne*

300

The Nymph's Reply

If all the world and love were young,
And truth in every shepherd's tongue,
These pretty pleasures might me move
To live with thee and be thy love.

But Time drives flocks from field to fold,
When rivers rage and rocks grow cold;
And Philomel becometh dumb;
The rest complain of cares to come.

The flowers do fade, and wanton fields
To wayward Winter reckoning yields:
A honey tongue, a heart of gall,
Is fancy's spring, but sorrow's fall.

Thy gowns, thy shoes, thy beds of roses,
Thy cap, thy kirtle, and thy posies,
Soon break, soon wither, soon forgotten,
In folly ripe, in reason rotten.

Thy belt of straw and ivy buds,
Thy coral clasps and amber studs—
All those in me no means can move
To come to thee and be thy love.

But could youth last, and love still breed;
Had joys no date, nor age no need;
Then those delights my mind might move
To live with thee and be thy love.

Sir Walter Raleigh

The Sphere of Glass

So through the sun-laced woods they went
Where no one walked but two that day,
And they were poets, and content
Sharing the one deep-vistaed way,
Sister and brother, to walk on
Where years like thickets round them lay.

It was the Roman dyke that ran
Between the bluebells and the fern,
The loam so fresh, they half began
To feel the bones deep under turn,
And, listening, dreamed their argument
Something from ancient death would learn.

One bird among the golden-green
Spangle of leaves was poised to sing:
They heard the opening trill, and then
Silence; as if its heart could bring
No note so pure but would disturb
The soundless fountain of the Spring.

Within the wood, within that hour
It seemed a sphere of glass had grown
That glittered round their lives with power
To link what grief the dyke had known
With voices of their vaster war
The sun-shot bombers homing drone,

And make one tragic harmony
Where still this theme, their hope, returned,
And still the Spring unchangeably
In fires of its own sap was burned
And poetry, from love and death,
The peace their human contest earned.

It might have been all history
Without the sphere of wonder lay
And just beyond their colloquy
Some truth more pure than they could say,
While through the bluebells and the fern
Sister and brother made their way.

John Lehmann

The Valley of the Elwy

I remember a house where all were good
To me, God knows, deserving no such thing:
Comforting smell breathed at very entering,
Fetched fresh, as I suppose, off some sweet wood.
That cordial air made those kind people a hood
All over, as a bevy of eggs the mothering wing
Will, or mild nights the new morsels of spring:
Why, it seemed of course; seemed of right it should.

Lovely the woods, waters, meadows, combes, vales,
All the air things wear that build this world of Wales;
Only the inmate does not correspond:
God, lover of souls, swaying considerate scales,
Complete thy creature dear O where it fails,
Being mighty a master, being a father and fond.

Gerard Manley Hopkins

Sonnet LVII: *"Being your slave, what should I do but tend"*

Being your slave, what should I do but tend
Upon the hours and times of your desire?
I have no precious time at all to spend,
Nor services to do, till you require.
Nor dare I chide the world-without-end hour
Whilst I, my sovereign, watch the clock for you.
Nor think the bitterness of absence sour
When you have bid your servant once adieu;
Nor dare I question with my jealous thought
Where you may be, or your affairs suppose,
But like a sad slave, stay and think of nought,
Save, where you are how happy you make those.
So true a fool is love that in your will
Though you do anything, he thinks no ill.

William Shakespeare

The Scrutinie

I

Why should you sweare I am forsworn,
   Since thine I vow'd to be?
Lady it is already Morn,
   And 'twas last night I swore to thee
That fond impossibility.

II

Have I not lov'd thee much and long,
   A tedious twelve houres space?
I must all other Beauties wrong,
   And rob thee of a new imbrace;
Could I still dote upon thy Face.

III

Not, but all joy in thy browne haire,
   By others may be found;
But I must search the black and faire
   Like skilfull Minerallist's that sound
For Treasure in un-plow'd-up ground.

IV

Then, if when I have lov'd my round,
   Thou prov'st the pleasant she;
With spoyles of meaner Beauties crown'd,
   I laden will returne to thee,
Ev'd sated with Varietie.

Richard Lovelace

Alba for Mélusine

"Et ades sera l'alba."
—Girautz de Bornelh

Waking beside you I watch this night
dissolve inexorable into dawn.
I put words from me. No need of second sight
to scotch the lie that seas are narrow,

305

years short and bring no change. No,
but the hand that grips your nape
shapes its degree of meaning
and blood-beat makes this alba for our parting:

Mélusine,
    may every other man ever to hold
you cool and agile in his arms
live forever—
up to the end of time and then beyond.
Death recede from him like the lake's level
from Tantalus. Coy oblivion elude him.
Aye, more: through unabridged eternity may he
grub fallow memory fruitless to conjure up
this smooth knoll of your shoulder,
this cwm of flank, this moss-delineated quite
un-Platonic cave.

May your feet's slenderness extort of him
arid invention
without reward of recollection.
May he recall you all amiss,
    that mat black wilful mane of yours
as aureate floss, your eyes
(which are obsidian) as chalcedony.
Even may he grope in vain to find the feral low
tonalities of your unprecedented voice in darkness.

That easy puma prowl of yours
come back to him as a mere human gait,
the tanbark scent of you be in his mind
only as some vague fragrancy
of heliotrope or lilac.

Mélusine,
may even the name he tries to suit
his spurious evocation to
forever evade his tongue.

For that, I leave this aubade, too, unsung.

                                    Ramon Guthrie

306

On a Dream

As Hermes once took to his feathers light,
  When lulled Argus, baffled, swoon'd and slept,
So on a Delphic reed, my idle spright
  So play'd, so charm'd, so conquer'd, so bereft
The dragon-world of all its hundred eyes;
  And seeing it asleep, so fled away,
Not to pure Ida with its snow-cold skies,
  Nor unto Tempe where Jove griev'd that day;
But to that second circle of sad Hell,
  Where in the gust, the whirlwind, and the flaw
Of rain and hail-stones, lovers need not tell
  Their sorrows—pale were the sweet lips I saw,
Pale were the lips I kiss'd, and fair the form
I floated with, about that melancholy storm.

                                        John Keats

Love Song: I and Thou

Nothing is plumb, level or square:
    the studs are bowed, the joists
are shaky by nature, no piece fits
    any other piece without a gap
or pinch, and bent nails
    dance all over the surfacing
like maggots. By Christ
    I am no carpenter. I built
the roof for myself, the walls
    for myself, the floors
for myself, and got
    hung up in it myself. I

307

danced with a purple thumb
   at this house-warming, drunk
with my prime whiskey: rage.
   Oh I spat rage's nails
into the frame-up of my work:
   it held. It settled plumb,
level, solid, square and true
   for that great moment. Then
it screamed and went on through,
   skewing as wrong the other way.
God damned it. This is hell,
   but I planned it, I sawed it,
I nailed it, and I
   will live in it until it kills me.
I can nail my left palm
   to the left-hand cross-piece but
I can't do everything myself.
   I need a hand to nail the right,
a help, a love, a you, a wife.

                              Alan Dugan

. . . Ask yourself my love whether you are not very cruel to have so entrammelled me, so destroyed my freedom. Will you confess this in the Letter you must write immediately and do all you can to console me in it—make it rich as a draught of poppies to intoxicate me—write the softest words and kiss them that I may at least touch my lips where yours have been. For myself I know not how to express my devotion to so fair a form: I want a brighter word than bright, a fairer word than fair. I almost wish we were butterflies and liv'd but three summer days—three such days with you I could fill with more delight than fifty common years could ever contain. But however selfish I may feel, I am sure I could never act selfishly. . . .

Letter from John Keats
to Fanny Brawne, 1 *July* 1819.

309

For a Dead Lady

No more with overflowing light
Shall fill the eyes that now are faded,
Nor shall another's fringe with night
Their woman-hidden world as they did.
No more shall quiver down the days
The flowing wonder of her ways,
Whereof no language may requite
The shifting and the many-shaded.

The grace, divine, definitive,
Clings only as a faint forestalling;
The laugh that love could not forgive
Is hushed, and answers to no calling;
The forehead and the little ears
Have gone where Saturn keeps the years;
The breast where roses could not live
Has done with rising and with falling.

The beauty, shattered by the laws
That have creation in their keeping,
No longer trembles at applause,
Or over children that are sleeping;
And we who delve in beauty's lore
Know all that we have known before
Of what inexorable cause
Makes Time so vicious in his reaping.

E. A. Robinson

"I have been faithful to thee, Cynara!
in my fashion"

Last night ah, yesternight, betwixt her lips and mine
There fell thy shadow, Cynara! thy breath was shed
Upon my soul between the kisses and the wine,
And I was desolate and sick of an old passion,
   Yea, I was desolate and bowed my head:
I have been faithful to thee, Cynara! in my fashion.

All night upon mine heart I felt her warm heart beat,
Night-long within mine arms in love and sleep she lay;
Surely the kisses of her bought red mouth were sweet;
But I was desolate and sick of an old passion,
   When I awoke and found the dawn was gray:
I have been faithful to thee, Cynara! in my fashion.

I have forgot much, Cynara! gone with the wind,
Flung roses, roses riotously with the throng,
Dancing, to put thy pale, lost lilies out of mind;
But I was desolate and sick of an old passion,
   Yea, all the time, because the dance was long:
I have been faithful to thee, Cynara! in my fashion.

I cried for madder music and for stronger wine,
But when the feast is finished and the lamps expire,
Then falls thy shadow, Cynara the night is thine;
And I am desolate and sick of an old passion,
   Yea hungry for the lips of my desire:
I have been faithful to thee, Cynara in my fashion.

Ernest Dowson

Elegy

Let them bury your big eyes
In the secret earth securely,
Your thin fingers, and your fair,
Soft, indefinite-coloured hair,—
All of these in some way, surely,
From the secret earth shall rise;
Not for these I sit and stare,
Broken and bereft completely:
Your young flesh that sat so neatly
On your little bones will sweetly
Blossom in the air.

But your voice . . . never the rushing
Of a river underground,
Not the rising of a wind
In the trees before the rain,
Not the woodcock's watery call,
Not the note the white-throat utters,
Not the feet of children pushing
Yellow leaves along the gutters
In the blue and bitter fall,
Shall content my musing mind
For the beauty of that sound
That in no new way at all
Ever will be heard again.

Sweetly through the sappy stalk
Of the vigourous weed,
Holding all it held before,
Cherished by the faithful sun,
On and on eternally

Shall your altered fluid run,
Bud and bloom and go to seed:
But your singing days are done;
But the music of your talk
Never shall the chemistry
Of the secret earth restore.
All your lovely words are spoken.
Once the ivory box is broken,
Beats the golden bird no more.

Edna St. Vincent Millay

11

". . . *Who lives*
Must learn to live his deaths. Who loves
Must learn the same."

Casabianca

Love's the boy stood on the burning deck
trying to recite "The boy stood on
the burning deck." Love's the son
   stood stammering elocution
     while the poor ship in flames went down.

Love's the obstinate boy, the ship,
even the swimming sailors, who
would like a schoolroom platform, too,
   or an excuse to stay
     on deck. And love's the burning boy.

Elizabeth Bishop

Lines supposed to have been addressed to Fanny Brawne

This living hand, now warm and capable
Of earnest grasping, would, if it were cold
And in the icy silence of the tomb,
So haunt thy days and chill thy dreaming nights
That thou would wish thine own heart dry of blood
So in my veins red life might stream again,
And thou be conscience-calm'd—see here it is—
I hold it towards you.

John Keats

316

The Dark and the Fair

A roaring company that festive night;
The beast of dialectic dragged his chains,
Prowling from chair to chair in the smoking light,
While the snow hissed against the windowpanes.

Our politics, our science, and our faith
Were whisky on the tongue; I, being rent
By the fierce divisions of our time, cried death
And death again, and my own dying meant.

Out of her secret life, that griffin-land
Where ivory empires build their stage, she came,
Putting in mine her small impulsive hand,
Five-fingered gift, and the palm not tame.

The moment clanged; beauty and terror danced
To the wild vibration of a sister-bell,
Whose unremitting stroke discountenanced
The marvel that the mirrors blazed to tell.

A darker image took this fairer form
Who once, in the purgatory of my pride,
When innocence betrayed me in a room
Of mocking elders, swept handsome to my side,

Until we rose together, arm in arm,
And fled together back into the world.
What brought her now, in the semblance of the warm,
Out of cold spaces, damned by colder blood?

317

That furied woman did me grievous wrong,
But does it matter much, given our years?
We learn, as the thread plays out, that we belong
Less to what flatters us than to what scars;

So, freshly turning, as the turn condones,
For her I killed the propitiatory bird,
Kissing her down. Peace to her bitter bones,
Who taught me the serpent's word, but yet the word.

Stanley Kunitz

February Loves

St. Valentine is gone with his sweet arts
that practice on St. Valentine's day.
How green our winter thoughts incarnate here
in cardboard chocolate and scarlet hearts
where courteous lovers put their loves away
in attics for another year.

Gone, gone the smiles, the pink wings, gone for good
love's cherubs with their silly little
bows. But our season's iconography
displays, a symbol dreaming in our blood,
the virgin of the forest pinned by brittle
glass arrows on a winter tree.

Richmond Lattimore

Wish for a Young Wife

My lizard, my lively writher,
May your limbs never wither,
May the eyes in your face
Survive the green ice
Of envy's mean gaze;
May you live out your life
Without hate, without grief,
And your hair ever blaze,
In the sun, in the sun,
When I am undone,
When I am no one.

Theodore Roethke

The Lovers

This painful love dissect to the last shred:
abjure it, it will not be solved in bed:
agony of the senses, but compounded
of soul's dream, heart's wish, blood's will, all confounded
with hate, despair, distrust, the fear of each
for what the other brings of alien speech.
Self-love, my love, no farther goes than this,
that when we kiss, it is ourselves we kiss.

O eyes no eyes, but fountains fraught with tears,
o heart no heart, but cistern of the years,
how backward now to childhood's spring we thrust
there to uncover the green shoots of lust:

how forward then to the bare skull we look
to taste our passion dead in doomsday book!
Self-love is all we know, my love, and this
breeds all these worlds, and kills them, when we kiss.

Yet would I give, yet would you take, a time
where self-love were no criminal, no crime:
where the true godhead in each self discovers
that the self-lovers are both gods and lovers.
O love, of this wise love no word be said,
it will be solved in a diviner bed,
where the divine dance teaches self-love this,
that when we kiss it is a god we kiss.

Conrad Aiken

The Clod and the Pebble

"Love seeketh not Itself to please,
Nor for itself hath any care,
But for another gives its ease,
And builds a Heaven in Hell's despair."

So sung a little Clod of Clay
Trodden with the cattle's feet,
But a Pebble of the brook
Warbled out these metres meet:

"Love seeketh only Self to please,
To bind another to Its delight,
Joys in another's loss of ease,
And builds a Hell in Heaven's despite."

William Blake

. . . Yesterday we were let out of Quarantine, during which my health suffered more from bad air and a stifled cabin than it had done the whole voyage. The fresh air revived me a little, and I hope I am well enough this morning to write to you a short calm letter;—if that can be called one, in which I am afraid to speak of what I would the fainest dwell upon. As I have gone thus far into it, I must go on a little;—perhaps it may relieve the load of WRETCHEDNESS which presses upon me. The persuasion that I shall see her no more will kill me. I cannot q____ My dear Brown, I should have had her when I was in health, and I should have remained well. I can bear to die—I cannot bear to leave her. Oh, God! God! God! Every thing I have in my trunks that reminds me of her goes through me like a spear. The silk lining she put in my travelling cap scalds my head. My imagination is horribly vivid about her—I see her—I hear her. There is nothing in the world of sufficient interest to divert me from her a moment. This was the case when I was in England; I cannot recollect, without shuddering, the time that I was prisoner at Hunt's, and used to keep my eyes fixed on Hampstead all day. Then there was a good hope of seeing her again—Now!—O that I could be buried near where she lives! I am afraid to write to her—to receive a letter from her—to see her hand writing would break my heart—even to hear of her any how, to see her name written would be more than I can bear. My dear Brown, what am I to do? Where can I look for consolation or ease? If I had any chance of recovery, this passion would kill me. Indeed through the whole of my illness, both at your house and at Kentish Town, this fever has never ceased wearing me out. . . .

Letter from John Keats
to Charles Brown, 1 November 1820, Naples.

Song from Aella

O sing unto my roundelay,
O drop the briny tear with me;
Dance no more at holyday,
Like a running river be!
  My love is dead,
   Gone to his death-bed
All under the willow-tree.

Black his cryne as the winter night,
White his rode as the summer snow,
Red his cheek as the morning light,
Cold he lies in the grave below:
  My love is dead,
   Gone to his death-bed
All under the willow-tree. . . .

Hark! the raven flaps his wing
In the briered dell below;
Hark! the death-owl loud doth sing
To the nightmares, as they go:
  My love is dead,
   Gone to his death-bed
All under the willow-tree.

See! the white moon shines on high;
Whiter is my true-love's shroud:
Whiter than the morning sky,
Whiter than the evening cloud:
  My love is dead,
   Gone to his death-bed
All under the willow-tree.

Here upon my true-love's grave
Shall the barren flowers be laid;
Not one holy saint to save
All the coldness of a maid:
   My love is dead,
    Gone to his death-bed
All under the willow-tree. . . .

Thomas Chatterton

Song for Afterwards

You who go every Sunday to the Botanical Garden
and while away hours in silence, contemplating
the sumptuous colourings of flowers
that you will never have in your own little garden;
you who ask fascinating things so ingenuously
and explain to me the fantastic ambient of your dreams;
you who love like a child the leaves of the mint
for the clean memories that its scent awakens;
you who talk about the glittering enamels
of exotic insects that blossom in the air;
you who tell the life of Jean-Jacques, and know
that under a clear sky he cuts herbs at close of day;
you who dress in white for the Month of Mary
and people the silence with images of peace:
because you were my beloved you will lay on my tomb,
when I am dead, lilacs of dark splendour.

Francisco Lopez Merino
Translated from the Spanish
by Richard O'Connell

"Filling her compact & delicious body"

Filling her compact & delicious body
with chicken páprika, she glanced at me
twice.
Fainting with interest, I hungered back
and only the fact of her husband & four other people
kept me from springing on her

or falling at her little feet and crying
'You are the hottest one for years of night
Henry's dazed eyes
have enjoyed, Brilliance.' I advanced upon
(despairing) my spumoni. —Sir Bones: is stuffed,
de world, wif feeding girls.

—Black hair, complexion Latin, jewelled eyes
downcast . . . The slob beside her   feasts . . . What wonders
   is
she sitting on, over there?
The restaurant buzzes. She might as well be on Mars.
Where did it all go wrong? There ought to be a law against Henry.
—Mr. Bones: there is.

John Berryman

Sestina of the Lady Pietra degli Scrovigni

To the dim light and the large circle of shade
I have clomb, and to the whitening of the hills,
There where we see no color in the grass.
Natheless my longing loses not its green,
It has so taken root in the hard stone
Which talks and hears as though it were a lady.

Utterly frozen is this youthful lady,
Even as the snow that lies within the shade;
For she is no more moved than is the stone
By the sweet season which makes warm the hills
And alters them afresh from white to green
Covering their sides again with flowers and grass.

When on her hair she sets a crown of grass
The thought has no more room for other lady,
Because she weaves the yellow with the green
So well that Love sits down there in the shade,—
Love who has shut me in among low hills
Faster than between walls of granite-stone.

She is more bright than is a precious stone;
The wound she gives may not be healed with grass:
I therefore have fled far o'er plains and hills
For refuge from so dangerous a lady;
But from her sunshine nothing can give shade,—
Not any hill, nor wall, nor summer-green.

A while ago, I saw her dressed in green,—
So fair, she might have wakened in a stone
This love which I do feel even for her shade;
And therefore, as one woos a graceful lady,
I wooed her in a field that was all grass
Girdled about with very lofty hills.

Yet shall the streams turn back and climb the hills
Before Love's flame in this damp wood and green
Burn, as it burns within a youthful lady,
For my sake, who would sleep away in stone
My life, or feed like beasts upon the grass,
Only to see her garments cast a shade.

How dark soe'er the hills throw out their shade,
Under her summer-green the beautiful lady
Covers it, like a stone cover'd in grass.

Cino Da Pistoia
*Translated from the Italian
by Dante Gabriel Rossetti*

A Broken Appointment

You did not come,
And marching Time drew on, and wore me numb,—
Yet less for loss of your dear presence there
Than that I thus found lacking in your make
That high compassion which can overbear
Reluctance for pure lovingkindness' sake
Grieved I, when, as the hope-hour stroked its sum,
You did not come.

You love not me,
And love alone can lend you loyalty;
—I know and knew it. But, unto the store
Of human deeds divine in all but name,
Was it not worth a little hour or more
To add yet this: Once you, a woman, came
To soothe a time-torn man; even though it be
You love not me?

Thomas Hardy

326

Neutral Tones

We stood by a pond that winter day,
And the sun was white, as though chidden of God,
And a few leaves lay on the starving sod;
    —They had fallen from an ash, and were gray.

Your eyes on me were as eyes that rove
Over tedious riddles of years ago;
And some words played between us to and fro
    On which lost the more by our love.

The smile on your mouth was the deadest thing
Alive enough to have strength to die;
And a grin of bitterness swept thereby
    Like an ominous bird a-wing. . . .

Since then, keen lessons that love deceives,
And wrings with wrong, have shaped to me
Your face, and the God curst sun, and a tree,
    And a pond edged with grayish leaves.

Thomas Hardy

To Diotima

Beautiful being, you live as do delicate blossoms in winter,
    In a world that's grown old hidden you blossom, alone.
Lovingly outward you press to bask in the light of the springtime,
    To be warmed by it still, look for the youth of the world.
But your sun, the lovelier world, has gone down now,
    And the quarreling gales rage in an icy bleak night.

Friedrich Hölderlin
*Translated from the German
by Michael Hamburger*

"What should I say"

What should I say,
Since faith is dead,
And truth away
From you is fled,
Should I be led
With doubleness?
Nay, nay, mistress!

I promised you,
And you promised me,
To be as true
As I would be.
But since I see
Your double heart,
Farewell my part!

Though for to take
It is not my mind,
But to forsake,
And as I find
So will I trust.
Farewell, unjust!

Can ye say nay?
But you said
That I always
Should be obeyed.
And thus betrayed
Or that I wist,
Farewell, unkissed.

Sir Thomas Wyatt

A *Birthday*

I never felt so much
Since I have felt at all
The tingling smell and touch
Of dogrose and sweet briar,
Nettles against the wall,
All sours and sweets that grow
Together or apart
In hedge or marsh or ditch.
I gather to my heart
Beast, insect, flower, earth, water, fire,
In absolute desire,
As fifty years ago.

Acceptance, gratitude:
The first look and the last
When all between has passed
Restore ingenuous good
That seeks no personal end,
Nor strives to mar or mend.
Before I touched the food
Sweetness ensnared my tongue;
Before I saw the wood
I loved each nook and bend,
The track going right and wrong;
Before I took the road
Direction ravished my soul.
Now that I can discern
It whole or almost whole,
Acceptance and gratitude
Like travellers return
And stand where first they stood.

Edwin Muir

"So, we'll go no more a-roving"

So, we'll go no more a-roving
   So late into the night,
Though the heart be still as loving,
   And the moon be still as bright.

For the sword outwears its sheath,
   And the soul wears out the breast,
And the heart must pause to breathe,
   And love itself have rest.

Though the night was made for loving,
   And the day returns too soon,
Yet we'll go no more a-roving
   By the light of the moon.

George Gordon, Lord Byron

"My lute awake!"

My lute awake! perform the last
Labor that thou and I shall waste,
   And end that I have now begun;
For when this song is sung and past,
   My lute be still, for I have done.

As to be heard where ear is none,
As lead to grave in marble stone,
   My song may pierce her heart as soon;
Should we then sigh, or sing, or moan?
   No, no, my lute, for I have done.

The rocks do not so cruelly
Repulse the waves continually,
   As she my suit and affection,
So that I am past remedy:
   Whereby my lute and I have done.

Proud of the spoil that thou hast got
Of simple hearts thorough love's shot,
   By whom, unkind, thou hast them won,
Think not he hath his bow forgot,
   Although my lute and I have done.

Vengeance shall fall on thy disdain,
That makest but game on earnest pain;
   Think not alone under the sun
Unquit to cause thy lovers plain,
   Although my lute and I have done.

Perchance thee lie withered and old,
The winter nights that are so cold,
   Plaining in vain unto the moon;
Thy wishes then dare not be told;
   Care then who list, for I have done.

And then may chance thee to repent
The time that thou hast lost and spent
   To cause thy lovers sigh and swoon;
Then shalt thou know beauty but lent,
   And wish and want as I have done.

Now cease, my lute, this is the last
Labor that thou and I shall waste,
   And ended is that we begun;
Now is this song both sung and past:
   My lute be still, for I have done.

Sir Thomas Wyatt

The Laboratory

ANCIEN RÉGIME

I

Now that I, tying thy glass mask tightly,
May gaze thro' these faint smokes curling whitely,
As thou pliest thy trade in this devil's-smithy—
Which is the poison to poison her, prithee?

II

He is with her, and they know that I know
Where they are, what they do: they believe my tears flow
While they laugh, laugh at me, at me fled to the drear
Empty church, to pray God in, for them!—I am here.

III

Grind away, moisten and mash up thy paste,
Pound at thy powder,—I am not in haste!
Better sit thus, and observe thy strange things,
Than go where men wait me and dance at the King's.

IV

That in the mortar—you call it a gum?
Ah, the brave tree whence such gold oozings come!
And yonder soft phial, the exquisite blue,
Sure to taste sweetly,—is that poison too?

V

Had I but all of them, thee and thy treasures,
What a wild crowd of invisible pleasures!
To carry pure death in an earring, a casket,
A signet, a fan-mount, a filigree basket!

VI

Soon, at the King's, a mere lozenge to give,
And Pauline should have just thirty minutes to live!
But to light a pastile, and Elise, with her head
And her breast and her arms and her hands, should drop dead!

VII

Quick—is it finished? The colour's too grim!
Why not soft like the phial's, enticing and dim?
Let it brighten her drink, let her turn it and stir,
And try it and taste, ere she fix and prefer!

VIII

What a drop! She's not little, no minion like me!
That's why she ensnared him: this never will free
The soul from those masculine eyes,—say, "no!"
To that pulse's magnificent come-and-go.

IX

For only last night, as they whispered, I brought
My own eyes to bear on her so, that I thought
Could I keep them one half minute fixed, she would fall
Shrivelled; she fell not; yet this does it all!

X

Not that I bid you spare her the pain;
Let death be felt and the proof remain:
Brand, burn up, bite into its grace—
He is sure to remember her dying face!

XI

Is it done? Take my mask off! Nay, be not morose;
It kills her, and this prevents seeing it close:
The delicate droplet, my whole fortune's fee!
If it hurts her, beside, can it ever hurt me?

XII

Now, take all my jewels, gorge gold to your fill,
You may kiss me, old man, on my mouth if you will!
But brush this dust off me, lest horror it brings
Ere I know it—next moment I dance at the King's!

Robert Browning

The Quarrel

Suddenly, after the quarrel, while we waited,
Disheartened, silent, with downcast looks, nor stirred
Eyelid nor finger, hopeless both, yet hoping
Against all hope to unsay the sundering word:

While the room's stillness deepened, deepened about us,
And each of us crept his thought's way to discover
How, with as little sound as the fall of a leaf,
The shadow had fallen, and lover quarrelled with lover;

And while, in the quiet, I marvelled—alas, alas—
At your deep beauty, your tragic beauty, torn
As the pale flower is torn by the wanton sparrow—
This beauty, pitied and loved, and now forsworn;

It was then, when the instant darkened to its darkest,—
When faith was lost with hope, and the rain conspired
To strike its gay arpeggios against our heartstrings,—
When love no longer dared, and scarcely desired:

It was then that suddenly, in the neighbor's room,
The music started: that brave quartette of strings
Breaking out of the stillness, as out of our stillness,
Like the indomitable heart of life that sings

When all is lost; and startled from our sorrow,
Tranced from our grief by that diviner grief,
We raised remembering eyes, each looked at other,
Blinded with tears of joy; and another leaf

Fell silently as that first; and in the instant
The shadow had gone, our quarrel became absurd;
And we rose, to the angelic voices of the music,
And I touched your hand, and we kissed, without a word.

                                              Conrad Aiken

"Kinde are her answeres"

Kinde are her answeres,
    But her performance keeps no day;
Breaks time, as dancers
    From their own Musicke when they stray:
    All her free favors and smooth words,
Wing my hopes in vaine.

335

O did ever voice so sweet but only fain?
   Can true love yeeld such delay,
   Converting joy to pain?

Lost is our freedome,
When we submit to women so:
Why doe wee neede them,
   When in their best they worke our woe?
   There is no wisedome
Can alter ends, by Fate prefixt.
O why is the good of man with evill mixt?
   Never were days yet cal'd two,
   But one night went betwixt.

                    Thomas Campion

The Echo Elf Answers

How much shall I love her?
For life, or not long?
     "Not long."

Alas! When forget her?
In years, or by June?
     "By June."

And whom woo I after?
No one, or a throng?
     "A throng."

Of these shall I wed one
Long hence, or quite soon?
     "Quite soon."

And which will my bride be?
The right or the wrong?
      "The wrong."

And my remedy—what kind?
Wealth-wove, or earth-hewn?
      "Earth-hewn."

                   Thomas Hardy

Ode I, 5: *To Pyrrha*

What slender youth, bedew'd with liquid odors,
Courts thee on roses in some pleasant cave,
     Pyrrha? For whom bind'st thou
     In wreaths thy golden hair,
Plain in thy neatness? O how oft shall he
Of faith and changed gods complain, and seas
     Rough with black winds, and storms
     Unwonted shall admire!
Who now enjoys thee credulous, all gold,
Who, always vacant, always amiable
     Hopes thee, of flattering gales
     Unmindful. Hapless they
To whom thou untried seem'st fair. Me, in my vow'd
Picture, the sacred wall declares to have hung
     My dank and dropping weeds
     To the stern god of sea.

              Horace
              Translated from the Latin
              by John Milton

The River-Merchant's Wife: A Letter

While my hair was still cut straight across my forehead
I played about the front gate, pulling flowers.
You came by on bamboo stilts, playing horse,
You walked about my seat, playing with blue plums.
And we went on living in the village of Chokan:
Two small people, without dislike or suspicion.

At fourteen I married My Lord you.
I never laughed, being bashful.
Lowering my head, I looked at the wall.
Called to, a thousand times, I never looked back.

At fifteen I stopped scowling,
I desired my dust to be mingled with yours
Forever and forever and forever.
Why should I climb the lookout?

At sixteen you departed.
You went into far Ku-to-yen by the river of swirling eddies,
And you have been gone five months.
The monkeys make sorrowful noise overhead.

You dragged your feet when you went out.
By the gate now, the moss is grown, the different mosses,
Too deep to clear them away!
The leaves fall early this autumn, in wind.
The paired butterflies are already yellow with August
Over the grass in the West garden;
They hurt me. I grow older.
If you are coming down through the narrows of the river Kiang,
Please let me know beforehand,
And I will come out to meet you
                    As far as Cho-fu-Sa.

                                        Li Po
                                        Translated from the Chinese
                                        by Ezra Pound

"Never seek to tell thy love"

Never seek to tell thy love
Love that never told can be;
For the gentle wind does move
Silently, invisibly.

I told my love, I told my love,
I told her all my heart,
Trembling, cold, in ghastly fears—
Ah, she doth depart.

Soon as she was gone from me
A traveller came by
Silently, invisibly—
O, was no deny.

William Blake

The Knife

Can I explain this to you? Your eyes
are entrances the mouths of caves—
I issue from wonderful interiors
upon a blessed sea and a fine day,
from inside these caves I look and dream.

Your hair explicable as a waterfall
in some black liquid cooled by legend
fell across my thought in a moment,
became a garment I am naked without,
lines drawn across through morning and evening.

And in your body each minute I died;
moving your thigh could disinter me
from a grave in a distant city:
your breasts deserted by cloth, clothed in twilight
filled me with tears, sweet cups of flesh.

Yes, to touch two fingers made us worlds,
stars, waters, promontories, chaos,
swooning in elements without form or time
come down through long seas among sea marvels
embracing like survivors on our islands.

This I think happened to us together
though now no shadow of it flickers in your hands,
your eyes look down on banal streets.
If I talk to you I might be a bird
with a message, a dead man, a photograph.

Keith Douglas

Porphyria's Lover

The rain set early in to-night,
    The sullen wind was soon awake,
It tore the elm-tops down for spite,
    And did its worst to vex the lake:
    I listened with heart fit to break.
When glided in Porphyria; straight

She shut the cold out and the storm,
And kneeled and made the cheerless grate
  Blaze up, and all the cottage warm;
  Which done, she rose, and from her form
Withdrew the dripping cloak and shawl,
   And laid her soiled gloves by, untied
Her hat and let the damp hair fall,
  And, last, she sat down by my side
  And called me. When no voice replied,
She put my arm about her waist,
  And made her smooth white shoulder bare,
And all her yellow hair displaced,
  And, stooping, made my cheek lie there,
  And spread, o'er all, her yellow hair,
Murmuring how she loved me—she
  Too weak, for all her heart's endeavour,
To set its struggling passion free
  From pride, and vainer ties dissever,
  And give herself to me for ever.
But passion sometimes would prevail,
  Nor could to-night's gay feast restrain
A sudden thought of one so pale
  For love of her, and all in vain:
  So, she was come through wind and rain.
Be sure I looked up at her eyes
  Happy and proud; at last I knew
Porphyria worshipped me; surprise
  Made my heart swell, and still it grew
  While I debated what to do.
That moment she was mine, mine, fair,
  Perfectly pure and good: I found
A thing to do, and all her hair
  In one long yellow string I wound
  Three times her little throat around,
And strangled her. No pain felt she;
  I am quite sure she felt no pain.

As a shut bud that holds a bee,
    I warily oped her lids: again
    Laughed the blue eyes without a stain.
And I untightened next the tress
    About her neck; her cheek once more
Blushed bright beneath my burning kiss:
    I propped her head up as before,
    Only, this time my shoulder bore
Her head, which droops upon it still:
    The smiling rosy little head,
So glad it has its utmost will,
    That all it scorned at once is fled,
    And I, its love, am gained instead!
Porphyria's love: she guessed not how
    Her darling one wish would be heard.
And thus we sit together now,
    And all night long we have not stirred,
    And yet God has not said a word!

                              Robert Browning

"Womanhood, wanton, ye want"

Womanhood, wanton, ye want:
    Your meddling, mistress, is mannerless;
Plenty of ill, of goodness scant,
    Ye rail at riot, reckless:
    To praise your port it is needless;
For all your draff yet and your dregs,
As well borne as ye full oft time begs.

Why so coy and full of scorn?
    Mine horse is sold, I ween, you say;
My new furrèd gown, when it is worn . . .

Put up your purse, ye shall not pay!
By crede, I trust to see the day,
As proud a pea-hen as ye spread,
Of me and other ye may have need!

Though angelic be your smiling,
    Yet is your tongue an adder's tail,
Full like a scorpion stinging
    All those by whom ye have avail.
    Good mistress Anne, there ye do shail:
What prate ye, pretty pigesnye?
I trust to 'quite you ere I die!

Your key is meet for every lock,
    Your key is common and hangeth out;
Your key is ready, we need not knock,
    Nor stand long wresting there about;
    Of your door-gate ye have no doubt:
But one thing is, that ye be lewd:
Hold your tongue now, all beshrewd!

To Mistress Anne, that farly sweet,
That wones at The Key in Thames Street.

John Skelton

Love in the Asylum

A stranger has come
To share my room in the house not right in the head,
    A girl mad as birds

Bolting the night of the door with her arm her plume.
    Strait in the mad bed
She deludes the heaven-proof house with entering clouds.

343

Yet she deludes with walking the nightmarish room,
    At large as the dead,
Or rides the imagined oceans of the male wards.

    She has come possessed
Who admits the delusive light through the bouncing wall,
    Possessed by the skies

She sleeps in the narrow trough yet she walks the dust
    Yet raves at her will
On the madhouse boards worn thin by my walking tears.

And taken by light in her arms at long and dear last
    I may without fail
Suffer the first vision that set fire to the stars.

                                        Dylan Thomas

God Wills It

The very earth will disown you
If your soul barter my soul;
In angry tribulation
The waters will tremble and rise.
My world become more beautiful
Since the day you took me to you,
When, under the flowering thorn tree
Together we stood without words,
And love, like the heavy fragrance
Of the flowering thorn tree, pierced us.

The earth will vomit forth snakes
If ever you barter my soul!
Barren of your child, and empty
I rock my desolate knees.

Christ in my breast will be crushed,
And the charitable door of my house
Will break the wrist of the beggar,
And repulse the woman in sorrow.

The kiss your mouth gives another
Will echo within my ear,
As the deep surrounding caverns
Bring back your words to me.
Even the dust of the highway
Keeps the scent of your footprints.
I track them, and like a deer
Follow you into the mountains.

Clouds will paint over my dwelling
The image of your new love.
Go to her like a thief, crawling
In the boweled earth to kiss her.
When you lift her face you will find
My face disfigured with weeping.

God will not give you the light
Unless you walk by my side.
God will not let you drink
If I do not tremble in the water.
He will not let you sleep
Except in the hollow of my hair.

If you go, you destroy my soul
As you trample the weeds by the roadside.
Hunger and thirst will gnaw you,
Crossing the heights or the plains;
And wherever you are, you will watch
The evenings bleed with my wounds.
When you call another woman
I will issue forth on your tongue,
Even as a taste of salt

Deep in the roots of your throat.
In hating, or singing, in yearning
It is me alone you summon.
If you go, and die far from me
Ten years your hand will be waiting
Hollowed under the earth
To gather the drip of my tears.
And you will feel the trembling
Of your corrupted flesh,
Until my bones are powdered
Into the dust on your face.

Gabriela Mistral
*Translated from the Spanish
by K.G.C.*

. . . Even when I am not thinking of you I receive your influence and a tenderer nature steeling upon me. All my thoughts, my unhappiest days and nights have I find not at all cured me of my love of Beauty, but made it so intense that I am miserable that you are not with me: or rather breathe in that dull sort of patience that cannot be called Life. I never knew before, what such a love as you have made me feel, was; I did not believe in it; my Fancy was affraid of it, lest it should burn me up. But if you will fully love me, though there may be some fire, 't will not be more than we can bear when moistened and bedewed with Pleasures. You mention 'horrid people' and ask me whether it depend upon them, whether I see you again—Do understand me, my love, in this—I have so much of you in my heart that I must turn Mentor when I see a chance of ha[r]m beffaling you. I would never see any thing but Pleasure in your eyes, love on your lips, and Happiness in your steps. I would wish to see you among those amusements suitable to your inclinations and spirits; so that our loves might be a delight in the midst of Pleasures agreeable enough, rather than a resource from vexations and cares—But I doubt much, in case of the worst, whether I shall be philosopher enough to follow my own Lessons: if I saw my resolution give you a pain I could not. Why may I not speak of your Beauty, since without that I could never have lov'd you—I cannot conceive any beginning of such love as I have for you but Beauty. There may be a sort of love for which, without the least sneer at it, I have the highest respect, and can admire it in others: but it has not the richness, the bloom, the full form, the enchantment of love after my own heart. So let me speak of you Beauty, though to my own endangering; if you could be so cruel to me as to try elsewhere its Power. You say you are affraid I shall think you do not love me—in saying this you make me ache the more to be near you. . . .

Letter from John Keats
to Fanny Brawne, 8 *July* 1819.

347

Little Elegy

Withouten you
No rose can grow;
No leaf be green
If never seen
Your sweetest face;
No bird have grace
Or power to sing;
Or anything
Be kind, or fair,
And you nowhere.

Elinor Wylie

"If I die"

If I die let my widow go
to Javel which is near Citron.
In a bistro she will find
at the sign of *le Beau Braun*

three musicians of a kind
who will play her—do si do—
the tune of pretty little Tane
who might have loved me once—who knows?

because a shade was all she offered
over the fiddles' rail and O
O my wife, o my November
underground the days are slow.

Jacques Audiberti
*Translated from the French
by William Mead*

348

The Expiration

So, so, breake off this last lamenting kisse,
   Which sucks two soules, and vapors Both away,
Turne thou ghost that way, and let mee turne this,
   And let our selves benight our happiest day,
We ask'd none leave to love; nor will we owe
   Any, so cheape a death, as saying, Goe;

Goe; and if that word have not quite kil'd thee,
   Ease mee with death, by bidding mee goe too.
Or, if it have, let my word worke on mee,
   And a just office on a murderer doe.
Except it be too late, to kill me so,
   Being double dead, going, and bidding, goe.

John Donne

On His Deceased Wife

Methought I saw my late espousèd Saint
   Brought to me like *Alcestis* from the grave,
   Whom *Jove's* great Son to her glad Husband gave,
   Rescu'd from death by force though pale and faint.
Mine as whom washt from spot of child-bed taint,
   Purification in the old Law did save,
   And such, as yet once more I trust to have
   Full sight of her in Heaven without restraint,
Came vested all in white, pure as her mind;
   Her face was vail'd, yet to my fancied sight,
   Love, sweetness, goodness, in her person shin'd
So clear, as in no face with more delight.
   But O as to embrace me she enclin'd
   I wak'd, she fled, and day brought back my night.

John Milton

From a Survivor

The pact that we made was the ordinary pact
of men & women in those days

I don't know who we thought we were
that our personalities
could resist the failures of the race

Lucky or unlucky, we didn't know
the race had failures of that order
and that we were going to share them

Like everybody else, we thought of ourselves as special

Your body is as vivid to me
as it ever was: even more

since my feeling for it is clearer:
I know what it could do and could not do

it is no longer
the body of a god
or anything with power over my life

Next year it would have been 20 years
and you are wastefully dead
who might have made the leap
we talked, too late, of making

which I live now
not as a leap
but a succession of brief, amazing movements

each one making possible the next

Adrienne Rich

12

"So preach to me, and tell me less of death
Than love that outlasts death,
as I've heard tell . . ."

Love

Of your lives and of your love
you gave, I took. And remembering how it was
I know you knew in all the years
of what you gave and what I took from you,
as who was young I never found you.

But now: if sometimes I only know the anguish of
too late this love that grows in me and reaches out
and you not here to take it—
is it how I think my way
to you who have the names of now the dead,

from your lives is how love comes to me.
And as it grows in me—
the way through me love reaches out to others:
am I old to learn it,
this love is yours and is the way I find you.

Pauline Hanson

Adam's Curse

We sat together at one summer's end,
That beautiful mild woman, your close friend,
And you and I, and talked of poetry.
I said: "A line will take us hours maybe;
Yet if it does not seem a moment's thought,
Our stitching and unstitching has been naught.
Better go down upon your marrow-bones
And scrub a kitchen pavement, or break stones
Like an old pauper, in all kinds of weather;
For to articulate sweet sounds together
Is to work harder than all these, and yet
Be thought an idler by the noisy set
Of bankers, schoolmasters, and clergymen
The martyrs call the world."

      And thereupon
That beautiful mild woman for whose sake
There's many a one shall find out all heartache
On finding that her voice is sweet and low
Replied: "To be born woman is to know—
Although they do not talk of it at school—
That we must labour to be beautiful."

I said: "It's certain there is no fine thing
Since Adam's fall but needs much labouring.
There have been lovers who thought love should be
So much compounded of high courtesy
That they would sigh and quote with learned looks
Precedents out of beautiful old books;
Yet now it seems an idle trade enough."

We sat grown quiet at the name of love;
We saw the last embers of daylight die,
And in the trembling blue-green of the sky
A moon, worn as if it had been a shell
Washed by time's waters as they rose and fell
About the stars and broke in days and years.

I had a thought for no one's but your ears:
That you were beautiful, and that I strove
To love you in the old high way of love;
That it had all seemed happy, and yet we'd grown
As weary-hearted as that hollow moon.

W. B. Yeats

"In my craft or sullen art"

In my craft or sullen art
Exercised in the still night
When only the moon rages
And the lovers lie abed
With all their griefs in their arms,
I labour by singing light
Not for ambition or bread
Or the strut and trade of charms
On the ivory stages
But for the common wages
Of their most secret heart.
Not for the proud man apart
From the raging moon I write
On these spindrift pages
Not for the towering dead
With their nightingales and psalms
But for the lovers, their arms

355

Round the griefs of the ages,
Who pay no praise or wages
Nor heed my craft or art.

Dylan Thomas

The Shape of Death

What does love look like?
Death is a cloud, immense
lid is lifted from the
clap of sound. A white
jaw of fright. A
white to gray, like a
and burns—then turns
away, filling the whole
Thickly it wraps, between
moon, the earth's green
cocoon, its choking
of death. Death is a

We know the shape of death.
and awesome. At first a
eye of light. There is a
blossom belches from the
pillared cloud churns from
monstrous brain that bursts
sickly black, spilling
sky with ashes of dread.
the clean seas and the
head. Trapped in its
breath, we know the shape
cloud. What does love look

like? Is it a particle,
beyond the microscope and
the length of hope? Is
that we shall never dare
color, and its alchemy?
can it be dug? Or
it be bought? Can it be
a shy beast to be caught?
a clap of sound. Love is
nests within each cell,
is a ray, a seed, a note,
our air and blood. It is
our very skin, a sheath

a star, invisible entirely,
Palomar? A dimension past
it a climate far and fair,
discover? What is its
Is it a jewel in the earth,
dredged from the sea? Can
sown and harvested? Is it
Death is a cloud—immense,
little and not loud. It
and it cannot be split. It
a word, a secret motion of
not alien—it is near—
to keep us pure of fear.

May Swenson

356

. . . You cannot conceive how I ache to be with you: how I would die for one hour——for what is in the world? I say you cannot conceive; it is impossible you should look with such eyes upon me as I have upon you: it cannot be. Forgive me if I wander a little this evening, for I have been all day employ'd in a very abstr[a]ct Poem and I am in deep love with you—two things which must excuse me. I have, believe me, not been an age in letting you take possession of me; the very first week I knew you I wrote myself your vassal; but burnt the Letter as the very next time I saw you I thought you manifested some dislike to me. If you should ever feel for Man at the first sight what I did for you, I am lost. Yet I should not quarrel with you, but hate myself if such a thing were to happen—only I should burst if the thing were not as fine as a Man as you are as a Woman. Perhaps I am too vehement, then fancy me on my knees, especially when I mention a part of you Letter which hurt me; you say speaking of Mr. Severn 'but you must be satisfied in knowing that I admired you much more than your friend.' My dear love, I cannot believe there ever was or ever could be any thing to admire in me especially as far as sight goes—I cannot be admired, I am not a thing to be admired. You are, I love you; all I can bring you is a swooning admiration of your Beauty. I hold that place among Men which snub-nos'd brunettes with meeting eyebrows do among women —they are trash to me—unless I should find one among them with a fire in her heart like the one that burns in mine. You absorb me in spite of myself—you alone: for I look not forward with any pleasure to what is call'd being settled in the world; I tremble at domestic cares—yet for you I would meet them, though if it would leave you the happier I would rather die than do so. I have two luxuries to brood over in my walks, your Loveliness and the hour of my death. O that I could have possession of them both in the same minute. . . .

Letter from John Keats
to Fanny Brawne, 25 July 1819.

Elegy

I

My comrade is dead.
In the assault confusion
parted us for a moment—
a moment, and now it is for ever!
I want to be alone,
hidden away from all eyes,
to make my lament.

II

How could I go on fighting
if I had clothed myself in valour
only because never in his presence
did I dare uncover
the natural weakness of my spirit?

III

Brother, and more than brother!
Now that you are gone from me,
my trappings weigh doubly upon me.
The icy wind is doubly cold.
If you could be the one to live, I the one who died!
Everything is so changed.

IV

Just as in the goblets at good feasts
the dark wine overflows
and leaves a red stain on the cloth,

your eyes overflowed with affection
and your face
was flooded with blushes.

V

Your glance
was sweeter than sleep and more soothing,
and better than dancing with women
was wrestling with you in the frost,
feeling your pure breath on my cheeks,
my whole body vibrating with your strength.

VI

Where can the maiden be—
predestined to a virgin widowhood—
whom your kiss, your kiss and no other man's,
should have made fruitful?
I would say to her: 'Sister,
take my body that was so much his
that though it does not bleed, it feels
the wound that gave his body rest!'

> Salomón de la Selva
> *Translated from the Spanish
> by Donald Walsh*

Sonnet CIV: *"To me, fair friend,
you never can be old"*

To me, fair friend, you never can be old,
For as you were when first your eye I eyed,
Such seems your beauty still. Three winters cold
Have from the forests shook three summers' pride,

Three beauteous springs to yellow autumn turned
In process of the seasons have I seen,
Three April perfumes in three hot Junes burned,
Since first I saw you fresh, which yet are green.
Ah, yet doth beauty, like a dial-hand,
Steal from his figure, and no pace perceived;
So your sweet hue, which methinks still doth stand,
Hath motion, and mine eye may be deceived:
For fear of which, hear this, thou age unbred;
Ere you were born was beauty's summer dead.

William Shakespeare

"Out of the rolling ocean the crowd"

Out of the rolling ocean the crowd came a drop gently to me,
Whispering, *I love you, before long I die,*
I have travell'd a long way merely to look on you to touch you,
For I could not die till I once look'd on you,
For I fear'd I might afterward lose you.

Now we have met, we have look'd, we are safe,
Return in peace to the ocean my love,
I too am part of that ocean, my love, we are not so much
    separated,
Behold the great rondure, the cohesion of all, how perfect!
But as for me, for you, the irresistible sea is to separate us,
As for an hour carrying us diverse, yet cannot carry us diverse
    forever;
Be not impatient—a little space—know you I salute the air, the
    ocean and the land,
Every day at sundown for your dear sake, my love.

Walt Whitman

Dark and Wrinkled

Dark and wrinkled like a deep pink,
It breathes, humbly nestled among the moss
Still wet with love that follows the gentle
Descent of the white buttocks to the edge of its border.

Filaments like tears of milk
Have wept under the cruel wind pushing them back
Over small clots of reddish marl,
And there lose themselves where the slope called them.

In my dream my mouth was often placed on its opening;
My soul jealous of the physical coitus,
Made of its fawny tear-bottle and its nest of sobs.

It is the fainting olive and the cajoling flute,
The tube from which the heavenly praline descends,
A feminine Canaan enclosed in moisture.

> Arthur Rimbaud
> *Translated from the French*
> *by Wallace Fowlie*

Sonnet LXXIII: *"That time of year thou mayst in me behold"*

That time of year thou mayst in me behold
When yellow leaves, or none, or few, do hang
Upon those boughs which shake against the cold,
Bare ruined choirs, where late the sweet birds sang.

In me thou see'st the twilight of such day
As after sunset fadeth in the west;
Which by and by black night doth take away,
Death's second self, that seals up all in rest.
In me thou see'st the glowing of such fire,
That on the ashes of his youth doth lie,
As the death-bed whereon it must expire,
Consumed with that which it was nourished by.
This thou perceivest, which makes thy love more strong,
To love that well which thou must leave ere long.

                                        William Shakespeare

Two in the Campagna

I

I wonder do you feel to-day
    As I have felt since, hand in hand,
We sat down on the grass, to stray
    In spirit better through the land,
This morn of Rome and May?

II

For me, I touched a thought, I know,
    Has tantalized me many times,
(Like turns of thread the spiders throw
    Mocking across our path) for rhymes
To catch at and let go.

Help me to hold it! First it left
   The yellowing fennel, run to seed
There, branching from the brickwork's cleft,
   Some old tomb's ruin: yonder weed
Took up the floating weft,

IV

Where one small orange cup amassed
   Five beetles,—blind and green they grope
Among the honey-meal: and last,
   Everywhere on the grassy slope
I traced it. Hold it fast!

V

The champaign with its endless fleece
   Of feathery grasses everywhere!
Silence and passion, joy and peace,
   An everlasting wash of air—
Rome's ghost since her decease.

VI

Such life here, through such lengths of hours,
   Such miracles performed in play,
Such primal naked forms of flowers,
   Such letting nature have her way
While heaven looks from its towers!

VII

How say you? Let us, O my dove,
　　Let us be unashamed of soul,
As earth lies bare to heaven above!
　　How is it under our control
To love or not to love?

VIII

I would that you were all to me,
　　You that are just so much, no more.
Nor yours nor mine, nor slave nor free!
　　Where does the fault lie? What the core
O' the wound, since wound must be?

IX

I would I could adopt your will,
　　See with your eyes, and set my heart
Beating by yours, and drink my fill
　　At your soul's springs,—your part my part
In life, for good and ill.

X

No. I yearn upward, touch you close,
　　Then stand away. I kiss your cheek,
Catch your soul's warmth,—I pluck the rose
　　And love it more than tongue can speak—
Then the good minute goes.

XI

Already how am I so far
   Out of that minute? Must I go
Still like the thistle-ball, no bar,
   Onward, whenever light winds blow,
Fixed by no friendly star?

XII

Just when I seemed about to learn!
   Where is the thread now? Off again!
The old trick! Only I discern—
   Infinite passion, and the pain
Of finite hearts that yearn.

Robert Browning

I Hear an Army

I hear an army charging upon the land,
And the thunder of horses plunging, foam about their knees:
Arrogant, in black armor, behind them stand,
Disdaining the reins, with fluttering whips, the charioteers.

They cry unto the night their battle-name:
I moan in sleep when I hear afar their whirling laughter.
They cleave the gloom of dreams, a blinding flame,
Clanging, clanging upon my heart as upon an anvil.

They come shaking in triumph their long, green hair:
They come out of the sea and run shouting by the shore.
My heart, have you no wisdom thus to despair?
My love, my love, my love, why have you left me alone?

James Joyce

Sonnet CXXIX: *"Th' expense of spirit in a waste of shame"*

Th' expense of spirit in a waste of shame
Is lust in action; and till action, lust
Is perjured, murderous, bloody, full of blame,
Savage, extreme, rude, cruel, not to trust;
Enjoy'd no sooner but despisèd straight;
Past reason hunted; and, no sooner had,
Past reason hated, as a swallow'd bait
On purpose laid to make the taker mad:
Mad in pursuit, and in possession so;
Had, having, and in quest to have, extreme;
A bliss in proof, and proved, a very woe,
Before, a joy proposed; behind, a dream.
All this the world well knows; yet none knows well
To shun the heaven that leads men to this hell.

William Shakespeare

"I remember you as you were that final autumn"

I remember you as you were that final autumn.
You were a gray beret and the whole being at peace.
In your eyes the fires of the evening dusk were battling,
and the leaves were falling in the waters of your soul.

As attached to my arms as a morning glory,
your sad, slow voice was picked up by the leaves.
Bonfire of astonishment in which my thirst was burning.
Soft blue of hyacinth twisting above my soul.

366

I feel your eyes travel and the autumn is distant:
gray beret, voice of a bird, and heart like a house
toward which my profound desires were emigrating
and my thick kisses were falling like hot coals.

The sky from a ship. The plains from a hill:
your memory is of light, of smoke, of a still pool!
Beyond your eyes the evening dusks were battling.
Dry leaves of autumn were whirling in your soul.

Pablo Neruda
*Translated from the Spanish
by Robert Bly*

Poem to be Read and Sung

I know there is someone
looking for me day and night inside her hand,
and coming upon me, each moment, in her shoes.
Doesn't she know the night is buried
with spurs behind the kitchen?

I know there is someone composed of my pieces,
whom I complete when my waist
goes galloping on her precise little stone.
Doesn't she know that money once out for her likeness
never returns to her trunk?

I know the day,
but the sun has escaped from me;
I know the universal act she performed in her bed
with some other woman's bravery and warm water, whose
shallow recurrence is mine.
Is it possible this being is so small
even her own feet walk on her that way?

A cat is the border between us two,

right there beside her bowl of water.
I see her on the corners, her dress—once
an inquiring palm tree—opens and closes . . .
What can she do but change her style of weeping?

But she does look and look for me. This is a real story!

César Vallejo
Translated from the Spanish
by James Wright and Robert Bly

From *Modern Love*

I: *"By this he knew she wept*
with waking eyes"

By this he knew she wept with waking eyes:
That, at his hand's light quiver by her head,
The strange low sobs that shook their common bed
Were called into her with a sharp surprise,
And strangled mute, like little gaping snakes,
Dreadfully venomous to him. She lay
Stone-still, and the long darkness flowed away
With muffled pulses. Then, as midnight makes
Her giant heart of Memory and Tears
Drink the pale drug of silence, and so beat
Sleep's heavy measure, they from head to feet
Were moveless, looking through their dead black years,
By vain regret scrawled over the blank wall.
Like sculptured effigies they might be seen
Upon their marriage-tomb, the sword between;
Each wishing for the sword that severs all.

VIII: *"Yet it was plain she struggled, and that salt"*

Yet it was plain she struggled, and that salt
Of righteous feeling made her pitiful.
Poor twisting worm, so queenly beautiful!
Where came the cleft between us? whose the fault?
My tears are on thee, that have rarely dropped
As balm for any bitter wound of mine:
My breast will open for thee at a sign!
But, no: we are two reed-pipes, coarsely stopped:
The God once filled them with his mellow breath;
And they were music till he flung them down,
Used! used! Hear now the discord-loving clown
Puff his gross spirit in them, worse than death!
I do not know myself without thee more:
In this unholy battle I grow base:
If the same soul be under the same face,
Speak, and a taste of that old time restore!

IX: *"He felt the wild beast in him betweenwhiles"*

He felt the wild beast in him betweenwhiles
So masterfully rude, that he would grieve
To see the helpless delicate thing receive
His guardianship through certain dark defiles.
Had he not teeth to rend, and hunger too?
But still he spared her. Once: 'Have you no fear?'
He said: 'twas dusk; she in his grasp; none near.
She laughed: 'No, surely; am I not with you?'
And uttering that soft starry 'you,' she leaned
Her gentle body near him, looking up;
And from her eyes, as from a poison-cup,
He drank until the flittering eyelids screened.
Devilish malignant witch! and oh, young beam

369

Of heaven's circle-glory! Here thy shape
To squeeze like an intoxicating grape—
I might, and yet thou goest safe, supreme.

XLIX: *"He found her by the ocean's moaning verge"*

He found her by the ocean's moaning verge,
Nor any wicked change in her discerned;
And she believed his old love had returned,
Which was her exultation, and her scourge.
She took his hand, and walked with him, and seemed
The wife he sought, though shadow-like and dry.
She had one terror, lest her heart should sigh,
And tell her loudly she no longer dreamed.
She dared not say, 'This is my breast: look in.'
But there's a strength to help the desperate weak.
That night he learned how silence best can speak
The awful things when Pity pleads for Sin.
About the middle of the night her call
Was heard, and he came wondering to the bed.
'Now kiss me, dear! it may be, now!' she said.
Lethe had passed those lips, and he knew all.

George Meredith

Love

In order to escape you,
stairs are no longer enough,
nor tunnels, nor airplanes,
telephones, nor ships.
All that accompanies
the man escaping:

silence, speech,
the trains and the years,—
avails not to flee
from this precise corner—
without clock or hours
or windows or pictures—
that goes with me
wherever I go.

In order to escape you
I need a weariness
born of you yourself:
a doubt or a rancour,
the shame of a weeping;
the fear that I felt
(for example) shaping
unfitly with my lips,
harsh and brusque,
your frail name. . . .

The hatred that I sensed
being born simultaneously
in you with our love,
will thrust me forth from your soul
sooner than light,
quicker than dream,
with greater precision
than the swiftest elevator:
the hatred which love
hides between its hands.

Jaime Torres Bodet
Translated from the Spanish
by Muna Lee de Muñoz Marín

Sonnet CXXXVIII: *"When my love swears that she is made of truth"*

When my love swears that she is made of truth,
I do believe her, though I know she lies,
That she might think me some untutored youth,
Unlearnéd in the world's false subtleties.
Thus vainly thinking that she thinks me young,
Although she knows my days are past the best,
Simply I credit her false-speaking tongue:
On both sides thus is simple truth suppressed.
But wherefore says she not she is unjust?
And wherefore say not I that I am old?
O, love's best habit is in seeming trust,
And age in love loves not to have years told:
Therefore I lie with her and she with me,
And in our faults by lies we flattered be.

William Shakespeare

The True Lover

The lad came to the door at night,
    When lovers crown their vows,
And whistled soft and out of sight
    In shadow of the boughs.

'I shall not vex you with my face
    Henceforth, my love, for aye;
So take me in your arms a space
    Before the east is grey.

'When I from hence away am past
    I shall not find a bride,
And you shall be the first and last
    I ever lay beside.'

She heard and went and knew not why;
    Her heart to his she laid;
Light was the air beneath the sky
    But dark under the shade.

'Oh do you breathe, lad, that your breast
    Seems not to rise and fall,
And here upon my bosom prest
    There beats no heart at all?'

'Oh loud, my girl, it once would knock,
    You should have felt it then;
But since for you I stopped the clock
    It never goes again.'

'Oh lad, what is it, lad, that drips
    Wet from your neck on mine?
What is it falling on my lips,
    My lad, that tastes of brine?'

'Oh like enough 'tis blood, my dear,
    For when the knife has slit
The throat across from ear to ear
    'Twill bleed because of it.'

                        A. E. Housman

Fire and Ice

Some say the world will end in fire,
Some say in ice.
From what I've tasted of desire
I hold with those who favor fire.
But if it had to perish twice,
I think I know enough of hate
To say that for destruction ice
Is also great
And would suffice.

Robert Frost

"The day is gone"

The day is gone, and all its sweets are gone!
    Sweet voice, sweet lips, soft hand, and softer breast,
Warm breath, light whisper, tender semi-tone,
    Bright eyes, accomplish'd shape, and lang'rous waist!
Faded the flower and all its budded charms,
    Faded the sight of beauty from my eyes,
Faded the shape of beauty from my arms,
    Faded the voice, warmth, whiteness, paradise—
Vanish'd unseasonably at shut of eve,
    When the dusk holiday—or holinight
Of fragrant-curtain'd love begins to weave
    The woof of darkness thick, for hid delight,
But, as I've read love's missal through to-day,
He'll let me sleep, seeing I fast and pray.

John Keats

"With how sad steps, o Moone, thou climb'st the skies"

With how sad steps, o Moone, thou climb'st the skies,
  How silently, and with how wanne a face,
  What may it be, that euen in heaunly place
  That busie archer his sharpe arrowes tries?

Sure if that long with *Loue* acquainted eyes
  Can judge of *Loue*, thou fee'st a Louers case;
  I read it in thy lookes, thy languisht grace,
  To me that feele the like, thy state descries.

Then ev'n of fellowship, o Moone, tell me.
  Is constant *Loue* deem'd there but want of wit?
  Are Beauties there as proud as here they be?

Do they above loue to be lou'd, and yet
  Those Louers scorne whom that *Loue* doth possesse?
  Do they call V*ertue* there ungratefulnesse?

                              Sir Philip Sidney

Forget Not Yet

Forget not yet the tried intent
Of such a truth as I have meant:
My great travail so gladly spent
          Forget not yet.

375

Forget not yet when first began
The weary life ye know, since whan
The suit, the service none tell can.
            Forget not yet.

Forget not yet the great assays,
The cruel wrong, the scornful ways,
The painful patience in denays.
            Forget not yet.

Forget not O, forget not this,
How long ago hath been, and is,
The mind that never meant amiss.
            Forget not yet.

Forget not then thine own approved,
The which so long hath thee so loved,
Whose steadfast faith yet never moved:
            Forget not this.

                            Sir Thomas Wyatt

To Fanny

I cry your mercy—pity—love!—aye, love!
    Merciful love that tantalizes not,
One-thoughted, never-wandering, guileless love,
    Unmask'd, and being seen—without a blot!
O! let me have thee whole,—all—all—be mine!
    That shape, that fairness, that sweet minor zest
Of love, your kiss,—those hands, those eyes divine,
    That warm, white, lucent, million-pleasured breast,—
Yourself—your soul—in pity give me all,
    Withhold no atom's atom or I die,

Or living on perhaps, your wretched thrall,
    Forget, in the mist of idle misery,
Life's purposes,—the palate of my mind
Losing its gust, and my ambition blind!

John Keats

Song: *"Why should a foolish marriage vow"*

I

Why should a foolish marriage vow,
    Which long ago was made,
Oblige us to each other now,
    When passion is decayed?
We loved, and we loved, as long as we could,
    Till our love was loved out in us both;
But our marriage is dead, when the pleasure is fled:
'Twas pleasure first made it an oath.

II

If I have pleasures for a friend,
    And further love in store,
What wrong has he, whose joys did end,
    And who could give no more?
'Tis a madness that he should be jealous of me,
    Or that I should bar him of another:
For all we can gain, is to give ourselves pain,
    When neither can hinder the other.

John Dryden

Sonnet: *"Upon a day, came Sorrow in to me"*
on the 9th of June 1290

Upon a day, came Sorrow in to me,
   Saying, 'I've come to stay with thee a while';
   And I perceived that she had ushered Bile
And Pain into my house for company.
Wherefore I said, 'Go forth—away with thee!'
   But like a Greek she answered, full of guile,
   And went on arguing in an easy style.
Then, looking, I saw Love come silently,
Habited in black raiment, smooth and new,
   Having a black hat set upon his hair;
And certainly the tears he shed were true.
   So that I asked, 'What ails thee, trifler?'
Answering he said: 'A grief to be gone through;
   For our own lady's dying, brother dear.'

> Dante Alighieri
> *Translated from the Italian*
> *by Dante Gabriel Rossetti*

The Skein

Moonlight through my gauze curtains
Turns them to nets for snaring wild birds,
Turns them into woven traps, into shrouds.
The old, restless grief keeps me awake.
I wander around, holding a scarf or shawl;
In the muffled moonlight I wander around
Folding it carefully, shaking it out again.

378

Everyone says my old lover is happy.
I wish they said he was coming back to me.
I hesitate here, my scarf like a skein of yarn
Binding my two hands loosely
      that would reach for paper and pen.

So I memorize these lines,
Dew on the scarf, dappling my nightdress also.
O love long gone, it is raining in our room!
So I memorize these lines,
      without salutation, without close.

                    Carolyn Kizer

From *Modern Love*

XLVIII: *"Their sense is with their senses all mixed in"*

Their sense is with their senses all mixed in,
Destroyed by subtleties these women are!
More brain, O Lord, more brain! or we shall mar
Utterly this fair garden we might win.
Behold! I looked for peace, and thought it near.
Our inmost hearts had opened, each to each.
We drank the pure daylight of honest speech.
Alas! that was the fatal draught, I fear.
For when of my lost Lady came the word,
This woman, O this agony of flesh!
Jealous devotion bade her break the mesh,
That I might seek that other like a bird.
I do adore the nobleness! despise
The act! She has gone forth, I know not where.
Will the hard world my sentience of her share?
I feel the truth; so let the world surmise.

379

XVI: *"In our old shipwrecked days there was an hour"*

In our old shipwrecked days there was an hour,
When in the firelight steadily aglow,
Joined slackly, we beheld the red chasm grow
Among the clicking coals. Our library-bower
That eve was left to us: and hushed we sat
As lovers to whom Time is whispering.
From sudden-opened doors we heard them sing:
The nodding elders mixed good wine with chat.
Well knew we that Life's greatest treasure lay
With us, and of it was our talk. 'Ah, yes!
Love dies!' I said: I never thought it less.
She yearned to me that sentence to unsay.
Then when the fire domed blackening, I found
Her cheek was salt against my kiss, and swift
Up the sharp scale of sobs her breast did lift:—
Now am I haunted by that taste! that sound!

George Meredith

A *Cameo*

There was a graven image of Desire
    Painted with red blood on a ground of gold
    Passing between the young men and the old,
And by him Pain, whose body shone like fire,
And Pleasure with gaunt hands that grasped their hire.
    Of his left wrist, with fingers clenched and cold,
    The insatiable Satiety kept hold,

Walking with feet unshod that pashed the mire.
The senses and the sorrows and the sins,
     And the strange loves that suck the breasts of Hate
Till lips and teeth bite in their sharp indenture,
Followed like beasts with flap of wings and fins.
     Death stood aloof behind a gaping grate,
Upon whose lock was written *Peradventure.*

Algernon Charles Swinburne

Bright Star

Bright star, would I were stedfast as thou art—
    Not in lone splendour hung aloft the night
And watching, with eternal lids apart,
    Like nature's patient, sleepless Eremite,
The moving waters at their priestlike task
    Of pure ablution round earth's human shores,
Or gazing on the new soft fallen mask
    Of snow upon the mountains and the moors—
No—yet still stedfast, still unchangeable,
    Pillow'd upon my fair love's ripening breast,
To feel for ever its soft fall and swell,
    Awake for ever in a sweet unrest,
Still, still to hear her tender-taken breath,
And so live ever—or else swoon to death.

John Keats

Market Women's Cries

APPLES

Come buy my fine wares,
Plums, apples and pears.
A hundred a penny,
In conscience too many:
Come, will you have any?
My children are seven,
I wish them in Heaven;
My husband 's a sot,
With his pipe and his pot,
Not a farthen will gain them,
And I must maintain them.

ONIONS

Come, follow me by the smell,
Here are delicate onions to sell;
I promise to use you well.
They make the blood warmer,
You'll feed like a farmer;
For this is every cook's opinion,
No savoury dish without an onion;
But, lest your kissing should be spoiled,
Your onions must be thoroughly boiled:
Or else you may spare
Your mistress a share,
The secret will never be known:
She cannot discover
The breath of her lover,
But think it as sweet as her own.

382

Be not sparing,
Leave off swearing.
Buy my herring
Fresh from Malahide,
Better never was tried.
Come, eat them with pure fresh butter and mustard,
Their bellies are soft, and as white as a custard.
Come, sixpence a dozen, to get me some bread,
Or, like my own herrings, I soon shall be dead.

Jonathan Swift

Dead Love

Dead love, by treason slain, lies stark,
White as a dead stark-stricken dove:
None that pass by him pause to mark
        Dead love.

His heart, that strained and yearned and strove
As toward the sundawn strives the lark,
Is cold as all the old joy thereof.

Dead men, re-arisen from dust, may hark
When rings the trumpet blown above:
It will not raise from out the dark
        Dead love.

Algernon Charles Swinburne

Rain on a Grave

Clouds spout upon her
  Their waters amain
  In ruthless disdain,—
Her who but lately
  Had shivered with pain
As at touch of dishonour
If there had lit on her
So coldly, so straightly
  Such arrows of rain:

One who to shelter
  Her delicate head
Would quicken and quicken
  Each tentative tread
If drops chanced to pelt her
  That summertime spills
  In dust-paven rills
When thunder-clouds thicken
  And birds close their bills.

Would that I lay there
  And she were housed here!
Or better, together
Were folded away there
Exposed to one weather
We both,—who would stray there
When sunny the day there,
  Or evening was clear
  At the prime of the year.

Soon will be growing
    Green blades from her mound,
And daisies be showing
    Like stars on the ground,
Till she form part of them—
Ay—the sweet heart of them,
Loved beyond measure
With a child's pleasure
    All her life's round.

Thomas Hardy

The Last Day and the First

The stocky woman at the door,
with her young daughter "Linda" looking
down, as she pulls out several copies
of *The Watchtower* from her canvas bag,
in a heavy German accent asks me:
"Have you ever thought that these
may be the last days of the world?"

And to my nodding "Yes, I have,"
she and the delicate, blonde girl
without a further word, turning tail,
sheepishly walk away.
                    And I feel
for them, as for us all, this world
in what may be its last days.
And yet this day itself is full
of unbelief, that or marvelously
convincing ignorance.

385

                                        Its young light
O so tentative, those first steps
as of a beginning dance (snowdrops
have already started up, and crocuses
we heard about last night the teller's
children quickly trampled in play)
make it hard not to believe that we are
teetering on creation's brink all over
again. And I almost thrill with fear
to think of what will soon be asked
of us, of you and me;
                                        am I at least
not a little old now (like the world)
to be trembling on the edge
of nakedness, a love, as Stendhal
knew it, "as people love for the first
time at nineteen and in Italy"?

Ah well, until I have to crawl
on hands and knees and then can crawl
no more, so may it every Italian-
returning season be, ever the last
day of this world about to burst
and ever for blossoming the first.

                                        Theodore Weiss

Song for the Last Act

Now that I have your face by heart, I look
Less at its features than its darkening frame
Where quince and melon, yellow as young flame,
Lie with quilled dahlias and the shepherd's crook.
Beyond, a garden. There, in insolent ease

The lead and marble figures watch the show
Of yet another summer loathe to go
Although the scythes hang in the apple trees.

Now that I have your face by heart, I look.

Now that I have your voice by heart, I read
In the black chords upon a dulling page
Music that is not meant for music's cage,
Whose emblems mix with words that shake and bleed.
The staves are shuttled over with a stark
Unprinted silence. In a double dream
I must spell out the storm, the running stream.
The beat's too swift. The notes shift in the dark.

Now that I have your voice by heart, I read.

Now that I have your heart by heart, I see
The wharves with their great ships and architraves;
The rigging and the cargo and the slaves
On a strange beach under a broken sky.
O not departure, but a voyage done!
The bales stand on the stone; the anchor weeps
Its red rust downward, and the long vine creeps
Beside the salt herb, in the lengthening sun.

Now that I have your heart by heart, I see.

Louise Bogan

Cracked Looking Glass

The tears, the firebursts and the vows,
The wild caprices and the bouts of pulse
The chills of sieged despairs, those flowers
Bought to match eyes and proffer aphrodisiacs
Of sighs and groans; the seizures.
World at the end of world when dusk falls slow
And all else but a taunting fast and loose.
Smooth skin, shut eyes and gliding limbs.

Love, I note you, stroke by stroke,
And show you how you play with shameless art
In the cracked looking glass that I hold up
What practice has made perfect, if it has.
The fits and starts, the going then to stay
The word, the gesture meant to take the heart
(If it be studied or be not)
Grand ceremonials of a play
By which we tried to live a passion out
By every nuance in a little room.
And cloistered so, tell out our stories
To pass the time until the moon rode high,
Improve upon the life we led,
Give gifts of praise, and so we did.
And if you postured in the looking glass
I made it for you, I held the witchery up
For you to see the secret life I guessed,
That more than improbable, celestial otherness.
And if you acted what I taught
Even as I learned it at your eyes
And your each ruse took on as if we borrowed
From every trick known to the over-wrought

And half-Platonic specialist,
We did it under moon craft or in twilight,
In all the half hours when the world becomes
All that imagination ever hoped it was.

My tear-quenched cost, I number half the ways
We chose a smoky vapor over fire
And tried to make a greater truth
Than what our contradictions could allow,
Exclaiming, as we breathed,
The true irrational.
And yet we were what we are.
And though the smoke is gone there is some fire
In saying so.

We made a play but not a discipline.
Love is the sternest master of the school.
But players tell a truth they cannot know.
They do not live it either, they enact
The fiery powers of instants in a light
Held up to them they cannot clarify.
Cease and be still. The pain is otherwise.
It's in the breaking face the clouds give to the moon
And in the flower that leans upon the air
Pouring its full life out into its scent.

Jean Garrigue

INDEX OF TITLES

INDEX OF FIRST LINES

(Asterisk denotes excerpt from Poem)

Being your slave, what should I do but tend, 304
Benedicite! whate dreamed I this nyght? 227
Body of a woman, white hills, white thighs, 24
Born of my voiceless time, your steps, 123
Bright star, would I were stedfast as thou art–, 381
But she had seen the cattle drop their young, 245
By night they haunted a thicket of April mist, 72
By this he knew she wept with waking eyes:* 368

Calling to mind, mine eye long went about, 121
Call it a good marriage–, 242
Can I explain this to you? Your eyes, 339
Clerk Saunders and may Margret, 76
Clouds spout upon her, 384
Come buy my fine wares, 382
Come, lecturer on love, resume your rostrum. 118
Come live with me, and be my love, 10
Come sleep! O sleep, the certain knot of peace, 185

Dark and wrinkled like a deep pink, 361
Dead love, by treason slain, lies stark, 383
Deare love, for nothing lesse then thee, 174
Dear, if you change, I'll never choose again; 231
Dear, why make you more of a dog than me? 212
Doing a filthy pleasure is, and short; 297

Elysium is as far as to, 271
Everything as before: blown snow, 143

Fain would I kiss my Julia's dainty Leg, 177
Famously she descended, her red hair, 21
Farewell, false love, the oracles of lies, 294
Farewell! thou art too dear for my possessing, 279
Farewell, thou child of my right hand, and joy, 221
Fiametta walks under the quincebuds, 201
Filling her compact & delicious body, 324
First time he kissed me, he but only kissed, 217
Fly to her heart; hover about her heart. 170
Forget not yet the tried intent, 375
Forgive me that I pitch your praise too low. 296

For Godsake hold your tongue, and let me love, 13
From a magician's midnight sleeve, 173
From Venus' breast a bit of greenery grows. 181
Full of her long white arms and milky skin, 252

Give me leave to rail at you, 56
God! how they plague his life, the three damned sisters, 275
God with honour hang your head, 242
Go, ill-sped book, and whisper to her or, 138
Go to the western gate, Luke Havergal, 140

Had we but world enough and time, 238
Happy ye leaves! when as those lily hands, 140
Having so rich a treasury, so fine a hoard, 104
Hearing that you would come who by my love, 190
He does not think that I haunt here nightly: 272
He felt the wild beast in him betweenwhiles,* 369
He found her by the ocean's moaning verge,* 370
Helpe me! helpe me! now I call, 75
Her body is not so white as, 16
'Holy Socrates, why always with deference, 136
How can I keep my maidenhead, 260
How do I love thee? Let me count the ways. 139
How happier is that flea, 9
How much shall I love her? 336
How shall I withhold my soul so that, 134
How sweet I roam'd from field to field, 33
How well you served me above ground, 185

I am my mammie's ae bairn, 168
I called you. You called me. 167
I cannot tell who loves the Skeleton, 39
I cry your mercy—pity—love!—aye, love! 376
I Dream'd we both were in a bed, 211
If all the world and love were young, 301
If, doubtful of your fate, 90
If I could send him only, 237
If I die let my widow go, 348
I figured you as nude between, 23
if i have made, my lady, intricate, 133

403

Love, love, a lily's my care, 94
"Love seeketh not Itself to please, 320
Love set you going like a fat gold watch. 246
Love's the boy stood on the burning deck, 316
Loving in truth, and fain in verse my love to show, 261
Lying asleep between the strokes of night, 107

Madame, withouten many words, 164
Man of himself's a little world, but join'd, 300
Meeting when all the world was in the bud, 251
Merry Margaret,/As midsummer flower, 178
Methought I saw my late espousèd Saint, 349
Me thought, (last night) love in an anger came, 108
Mine—by the Right of the White Election! 186
Moonlight through my gauze curtains, 378
Most near, most dear, most loved and most far, 250
Mouth to mouth joined we lie, her naked breasts, 269
My comrade is dead. 358
My girl, thou gazest much, 7
My lizard, my lively writher, 319
My love, I have betrayed you seventy times, 277
My love is of a birth as rare, 6
My lovers suffocate me, 11
My lute awake! perform the last, 330
My pillow won't tell me: 124
My sweetest Lesbia, let us live and love, 106
My true Love hath my heart, and I have his, 130

Never give all the heart, for love, 122
Never seek to tell thy love, 339
No longer itself, 172
No more with overflowing light, 310
No one can die twice of the same fever? 236
Not at midnight, not at morning, O sweet city, 226
Nothing is plumb, level or square: 307
Not yet can she bear the yoke on submissive neck, 49
Now I am slow and placid, fond of sun, 243
Now sleeps the crimson petal, now the white;* 214
Now that I have your face by heart, I look, 386

Now that I, tying thy glass mask tightly, 332
Nymphs and shepherds dance no more, 215

Of all the Souls that stand create—, 105
Of your lives and of your love, 353
Oh do not wanton with those eyes, 62
Oh, with the hunger of the sea, forever born anew, 12
O kiss me yet again, O kiss me over, 193
O my dark Rosaleen, 247
One day I wrote her name upon the strand, 41
One that is ever kind said yesterday: 228
On the long shore, lit by the moon, 261
O sing unto my roundelay, 322
O the opal and the sapphire of that wandering western sea, 218
Out of the rolling ocean the crowd came a drop gently to me, 360
O what can ail thee, knight-at-arms, 112
O where is the dwelling I love the most, 285

Pack, clouds, away! and welcome day! 236
Peer of the golden gods is he to Sappho, 217
Put your head, darling, darling, darling, 55

Queer are the ways of a man I know: 268

Refusing to fall in love with God, he gave, 195
Return often and take me, 107
Round the cape of a sudden came the sea, 184

See the Chariot at hand here of Love, 20
Shall I come, sweet Love, to thee, 88
Shelter was possible. Instead, 17
SHEPHEARD, what's Loue, I pray thee tell? 142
She speaks always in her own voice, 61
She stepped two paces forward, 126
Since there's no help, come let us kiss and part—, 285
Since this is the last night I keep you home. 8
Skirting the river road (my forenoon walk, my rest), 61
Some day, when I lose you, 86
Some say the world will end in fire, 374
somewhere i have never travelled, gladly beyond, 288

So, so, breake off this last lamenting kisse, 349
So through the sun-laced woods they went, 302
So, we'll go no more a-roving, 330
Strange fits of passion have I known: 230
St. Valentine is gone with his sweet arts, 318
Suddenly, after the quarrel, while we waited, 334
Surprised by joy—impatient as the Wind, 186
Sylvia the fair, in the bloom of fifteen, 198

That her serene influence should spread, 286
That time of year thou mayst in me behold, 361
The animal moment, when he sorted out her tail, 13
The day is gone, and all its sweets are gone! 374
The fitter said, "Madame, vous avez maigri.", 298
The government of your body, sweet, 59
The grey sea and the long black land; 184
Their sense is with their senses all mixed in,* 379
The lad came to the door at night, 372
The lark now leaves his watery nest, 177
The moon was born grey, and Beethoven was weeping, 274
The nightingale has a lyre of gold, 213
The pact that we made was the ordinary pact, 350
The rain set early in to-night, 340
There came a Day at Summer's full, 111
There came you wishing me ***, 36
There is a Lady sweet and kind, 196
There is a myth, a tale men tell: 124
There is a white mare that my love keeps, 180
There was a graven image of Desire, 380
The stocky woman at the door, 385
The tears, the firebursts and the vows, 388
The very earth will disown you, 344
The Way I read a Letter's—this—, 163
The wind blew all my wedding-day, 110
Th' expense of spirit in a waste of shame, 366
They amputated/Your thighs off my hips. 244
They flee from me that sometime did me seek, 222
They that have power to hurt and will do none, 165
This living hand, now warm and capable, 316
This painful love dissect to the last shred: 319

407

Where, like a pillow on a bed, 26
While my hair was still cut straight across my forehead, 338
Whil'st *Alexis* lay prest, 171
Who is she coming, whom all gaze upon, 25
Who on your breast pillows his head now, 199
Who shall have my faire lady? 12
Why art thou silent! Is thy love a plant, 228
Why dost thou shade thy lovely face? O why, 137
Why should a foolish marriage vow, 377
Why should you sweare I am forsworn, 304
Wild Nights—Wild Nights! 32
Will you perhaps consent to be, 264
Wine comes in at the mouth, 66
With how sad steps, o Moone, thou climb'st the skies, 375
With lullay, lullay, like a child, 207
With my frailty, don't upbraid me, 211
Withouten you/No rose can grow; 348
With thee, in the Desert—, 26
Wo'd I see Lawn, clear as the Heaven, and thin? 170
Womanhood, wanton, ye want: 342

Ye learnèd sisters, which have oftentimes, 145
Yet it was plain she struggled, and that salt,* 369
You are already/asleep. I lower, 256
You did not come, 326
You must live through the time when everything hurts, 277
You say, to me-wards your affection's strong; 91
"You say you love me truly, 63
You shun me, Chloë, wild and shy, 49
You who go every Sunday to the Botanical Garden, 323

AUTHOR INDEX

Each entry identifies the poet by nationality and indicates the century or centuries of greatest literary productivity.

Gunn, Thom. 20th century. English. 256

Guthrie, Ramon. 20th century. American. 305

H.D. (Hilda Doolittle). 20th century. American. 201

Hanson, Pauline. 20th century. American. 353

Hardy, Thomas. 19–20th centuries. English. 209, 218, 268, 272, 293, 326, 327, 336, 384

Henley, William Ernest. 19th century. English. 213

Herbert, George. 17th century. English. 194

Herrick, Robert. 17th century. English. 11, 75, 91, 108, 170, 177, 211

Heywood, Thomas. 17th century. English. 236

Hölderlin, Friedrich. 18–19th centuries. German. 136, 327

Hopkins, Gerard Manley. 19th century. English. 242, 303

Horace (Quintus Horatius Flaccus). 1st century, B.C. Latin (Roman). 49, 213, 337

Housman, A. E. (Alfred Edward). 19–20th centuries. English. 120, 372

Howard, Henry, Earl of Surrey. 16th century. English. 89

Huidobro, Vincente. 20th century. Chilean. 126

Hutchinson, Robert. 20th century. American. 265

Jacob, Max. 20th century. French. 51

Jiménez, Juan Ramón. 20th century. Spanish. 205, 274

Jonson, Ben(jamin). 17th century. English. 20, 62, 221, 297

Joyce, James. 20th century. Irish. 365

Keats, John. 19th century. English. 19, 67, 86, 99, 112, 144, 203, 225, 240, 307, 309, 316, 321, 347, 357, 374, 376, 381

Kinnell, Galway. 20th century. American. 182

Kizer, Carolyn. 20th century. American. 378

Knight of Kürenberg. Medieval. German. 182

Kunitz, Stanley. 20th century. American. 317

Labé, Louise (known as la Belle Cordière). 16th century. French. 180, 193

Laforgue, Jules. 19th century. French. 258

Larbaud, Valery. 20th century. French. 125, 270

Larkin, Philip. 20th century. English. 110

Lattimore, Richmond. 20th century. American. 318

Lawrence, D. H. (David Herbert). 20th century. English. 8, 42

Lehmann, John. 20th century. English. 302

Li Po. 8th century. Chinese. 338

Lorca, Federico García. 20th century. Spanish. 68